PLANTS
TASTE
BETTER

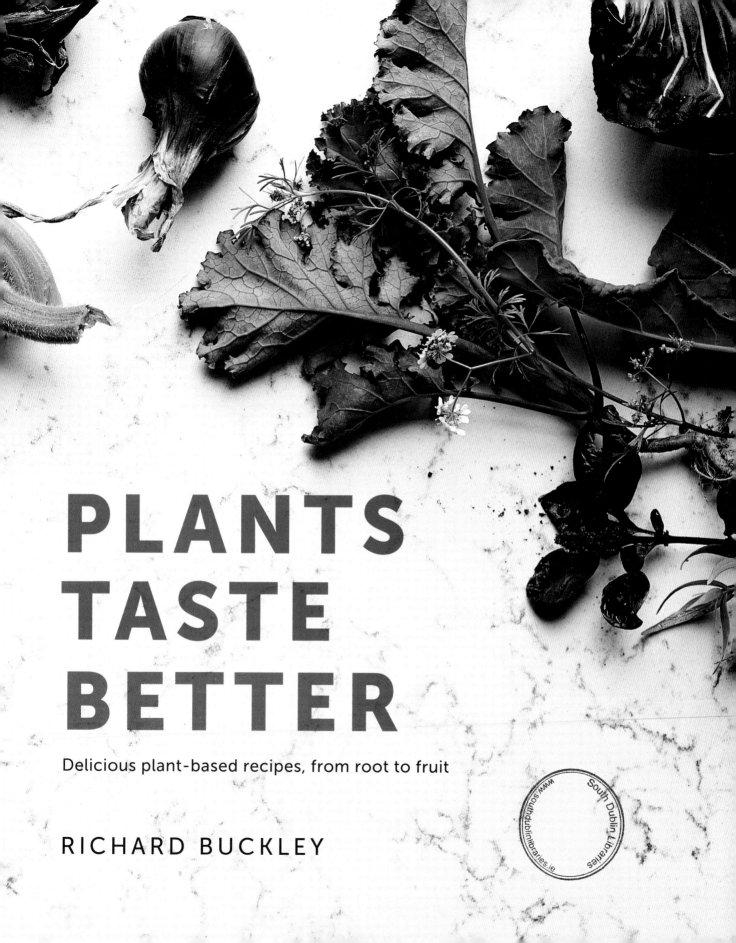

PLANTS
TASTE
BETTER

Delicious plant-based recipes, from root to fruit

RICHARD BUCKLEY

For Helen – the reason for everything

Quarto is the authority on a wide range of topics.
Quarto educates, entertains and enriches the lives of
our readers – enthusiasts and lovers of hands-on living.
www.QuartoKnows.com

Design, layout and photography copyright
© 2018 Quarto Publishing Group plc
Text copyright © Richard Buckley

First published in 2018 by Jacqui Small
an imprint of The Quarto Group.
The Old Brewery, 6 Blundell Street
London N7 9BH, United Kingdom.
T (0)20 7700 6700 F (0)20 7700 8066
www.QuartoKnows.com

Publisher: Jacqui Small
Senior Commissioning Editor: Fritha Saunders
Managing Editor: Emma Heyworth-Dunn
Production: Maeve Healy
Designer: Tania Gomes
Photographer: Kim Lightbody
Editor: Claire Wedderburn-Maxwell

ISBN: 978-1-911127-32-1

A catalogue record for this book is available from
the British Library.

2020 2019 2018
10 9 8 7 6 5 4 3 2 1

Printed in China

CONTENTS

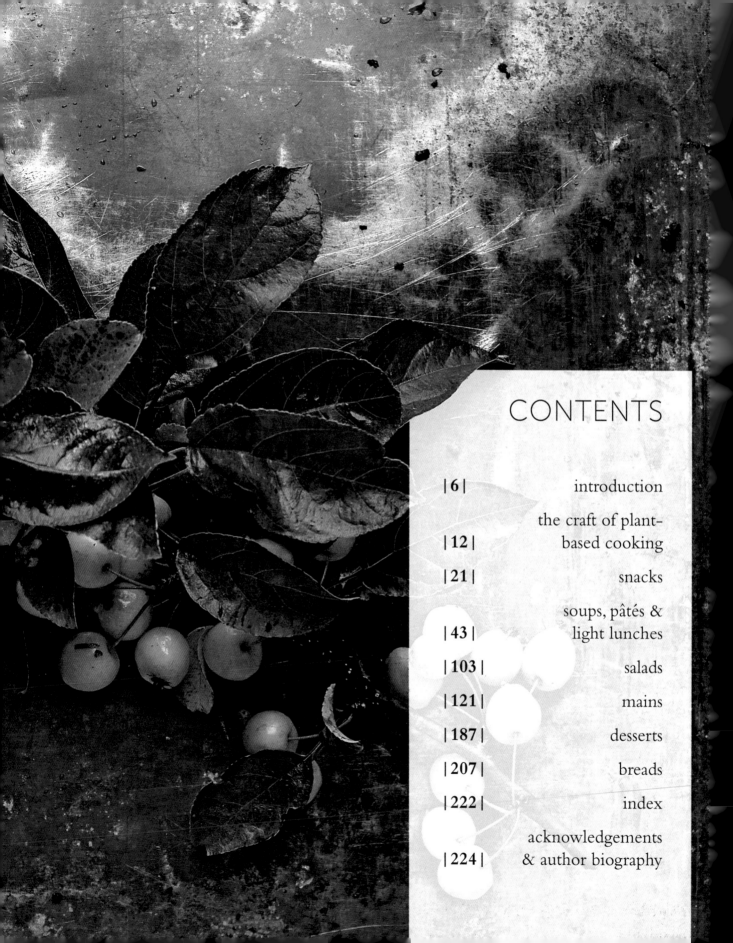

INTRODUCTION

cooking with plants

We've all cooked plants before, be it boiling a carrot, baking a loaf of bread or brewing a cup of coffee. There is nothing special about it, but it does require care to produce the best results. Plants and fungi are amazing organisms and they make up the majority of the flavours in our diet. Think of any dish – from a curry to the most complex Michelin-starred meal – and I can guarantee that most of the flavours come from plants. I have spent 15 years studying plants as food, how they fit into our culture and how to get the most out of them. Over time I found many wonderful techniques and realized that I was producing the best flavours when I focused on the plants, not on the animals, or lack of.

This book is not a manual, it is a series of practical examples for cooking plants carefully and with skill at home, taking into consideration the raw ingredient itself, the craft traditions that surround it and the culinary principles of fine cookery. It is not necessary to cook every recipe or to cook every part of every plate of food, but I hope the idea that plants can be cooked with grace will permeate through everything you produce and will influence the way that you look at plants from that point onwards.

understanding plants

Take a carrot and hold it in your hand. It's a carrot, right? Yes, but before that it is a root vegetable and before that it is part of a plant. Broadly speaking, all plants are the same. They have roots in the ground, stems to connect and support the various parts, leaves to capture the energy from the sun, flowers to help them reproduce, and fruits and seeds to create more plants the same as themselves. There is infinite variety within this, but the structure remains the same.

When we talk of a vegetable, herb, fruit or seed we are really just talking about a part of a plant that, either through chance or cultivation, we find is well suited to our diet and culinary traditions. We eat plant parts that share similar characteristics. We only eat taproots that swell with sugars and starches to provide energy for the next year. We don't eat the spindly or woody roots of grass or hazel trees. We eat the leaves that are large and mild in flavour as salads, and those that are small and strongly flavoured as herbs. The seeds surrounded by fruits we call nuts, and those that come from pods we call beans. Those that are small and intense in flavour we call spices, and those that are high in starches we call grains.

The ingenuity and craft traditions that have emerged and evolved over the centuries in our treatment of plants are for me some of the fascinations and deep pleasures of cookery: from stone-grinding flour to fermenting cabbage, the connection of the cook to the ingredient, and through it the processes of the natural world, are a source of endless wonder. That said, these traditional processes tend to make use of the same characteristics of the plant part they are using and we tend to use the same techniques for each part of the plant. We roast nuts and seeds to release their intense flavours: there is little difference between roasting almonds

and toasting cumin in terms of what we are trying to achieve and the methods we are using. We cook beans and grains with water to hydrate and modify the starches and make them more digestible; soaking and boiling beans is essentially the same process as combining water with flour and baking it to make bread – you are hydrating and heating. We slice stems across their width to break the chewy fibres that give them strength as a plant and we cook leaves lightly to preserve their delicate colour and structure. An in-depth examination of each plant part and the best cooking techniques for them is well beyond the scope of this book; however, your cooking will improve instantly and for ever if you simply begin to think of the ingredients in front of you as parts of a plant with certain characteristics and the cooking technique merely as a way of enhancing and manipulating those characteristics to suit our appetites and those of our guests.

root to fruit

We waste so many ingredients in the kitchen. People who throw the core from a broccoli or cauliflower in the bin are losing one of the best parts of the vegetable. Carrot tops are lovely and grassy as a herb, and fennel fronds make the best garnish there is. Trying to apply the nose-to-tail philosophy popular in butchery doesn't quite work for plants as parts of some of them are poisonous, such as the leaves of rhubarb or the almond-like stones of apricots. Another issue is that we have developed the varieties of plants we eat over generations of selective breeding so there is very little wild about them. The shoots on the top of a celeriac (celery root) are a celery of sorts, and they are great in a stock, but true celery has been bred to be less woody and stringy. They are the same thing but with a different emphasis. The same can be said of beetroot (beet) tops: they can be cooked but have a much stronger iron flavour than the varieties that are bred for the leaf with a spindly little root at the bottom.

I believe that if a vegetable has multiple edible parts then it is a crime to simply throw a bit away because it is not the part you want. A great many recipes in here follow that philosophy implicitly. My cauliflower hearts dish (see page 176) was designed to use the whole cauliflower head, not because it's trendy but because it's the right thing to do. If you are lucky enough to get your cauliflower surrounded by the leaves you can even use these in place of the kale in the purée. If your beetroot (beets) have leaves on them, keep them and sauté them as an extra garnish. If your fennel in the garden has bolted and gone to seed, wait for the fresh seeds to emerge and harvest them for the freshest, cleanest aniseed flavour you've ever tasted. Sprinkled over a poached pear, they are a revelation.

keep it in the family

Most plants that look the same are from the same family. Almonds, apricots, peaches and cherries all share an ancestor or three. Almonds became as prized for their seed as the others did for their flesh. Some are less obvious – tomatoes, potatoes and aubergines (eggplants) are all members of the nightshade family. Thinking of them in this way can help you to break down the cultural bias you have around a plant and see it in a new light. Courgettes (zucchini) are related to pumpkin, melon and cucumber, and considering them as part of that family breaks them from the ratatouille-shaped box they probably live in. Carrots, fennel, cumin, parsley and celery are all umbellifers, their seeds, roots, flowers and leaves all relate wonderfully to each other and create some really interesting harmonies and substitutions. Rhubarb and buckwheat anyone? Jerusalem artichoke and sunflower seeds? Once you start to think of plants in this way the connections are endless.

THE CRAFT OF PLANT-BASED COOKING

choosing your ingredients

It is almost a cliché but the dishes you make will only taste of what you put in them. The greatest chef in the world cannot make the red balls of foam that appear in supermarkets in the depths of the English winter labelled "tomatoes" taste like anything worth eating.

Organic is better than non-organic, but the label is not important. When you eat a plant you are eating an entire ecosystem, the minerals and flavours in an ingredient come from the land it is grown in and the air that surrounds it. The organic movement has helped to push real farming techniques to the fore, but what really matters is the care of the soil. I would rather buy vegetables from a small grower at a farmers' market who cares for and respects their soil, but cannot afford an organic certification, than I would organic produce from a supermarket that is grown in a big sterile monoculture. Remember organic is focused on what chemicals *aren't* used in growing, not on the positive growing techniques used. Going to your local market allows you to meet the growers and find out how they grow their crops. If they talk about soil more than yield, you know you are on to a winner. You do need to use your own judgement though; just because they are a small producer using organic methods it does not mean they are a skilled grower. The organic movement does attract a number of growers whose enthusiasm for the ethics exceeds their love of the plants. If their produce is poor quality then no amount of good intention is going to make up for it and you are better off in a decent supermarket.

It feels unnecessary to say in this day and age, but it is rarely worth buying plants out of their season. You may be able to buy strawberries and peaches in the winter but there is little point to them, they taste of nothing and often have a strange texture. If you know that something is not at its best then it is best not to buy it.

I have chosen the recipes in this book so that you can find nearly all the ingredients you need in your local supermarket. I would rather focus on the skill and technique of cooking than showing off obscure ingredients no one can find. However, I would encourage you to leave the safety of the aisles if you can and support and meet your local farmers and growers. Your food will taste better and will have whole new layers of meaning as you connect the person who grew the ingredients and the land they did it on to the food on your plate.

flavour and taste

We often use the terms "flavour" and "taste" interchangeably, but they are different things. I think of flavour as the combined experience of the aroma of the food experienced retronasally, through the back of the nose, and the taste of the food in the mouth. Taste is those experiences that happen within the mouth – the recognized five tastes: salt, sweet, acidic, bitter and umami, as well as the emerging recognition of a fat taste and also astringency (the heat of chilli and mustard).

You need to balance the tastes of a dish making sure the elements are all in check and nothing stands out unless it needs to, as in the acidity of pickles. I always think of taste like the rhythm section of a blues band, you need the drive and groove before you scatter the aromas, the melody, over the top. You can use one taste to balance another; for example, sweetness will balance bitterness, but so will salt. Acidity will balance an overly salty dish and bitterness will add interest to an overly sweet food. This art is complex and my only advice is to trust your instincts and to eat lots of fine food so you can learn instinctively where the "sweet spot" is. People who eat a lot of junk food tend to balance food to taste like junk food, with high salt, sugar and acidity. When matching flavours and aromas, the general rule is "like matches like" – foods that go well together tend to share common aroma compounds.

seasoning with salt

Seasoning is probably the single most important cooking skill you can master, and often the most misunderstood. Salt should not be thought of as a flavour in itself, unless you are putting it on top of breads or crackers. Instead it is generally used as a flavour enhancer, a way of drawing out the flavour of the ingredients in the dish. When a recipe says "season to taste" it does not mean "add salt to your liking", it means "taste the food and add salt until you have achieved the correct flavour balance". Broadly speaking, this amount is objective – there is a correct amount of salt. There may be slight differences in the amount of salt people can biologically taste, but it is a small percentage difference, not the difference between the small pinch my mum adds (who has heard that too much salt is bad for you), and the spoonfuls a young chef may add. When seasoning you are looking for the flavours to come alive, to be bright and vibrant and to feel full in the mouth. As a rule of thumb, if a dish tastes thin and watery, it needs more salt; if you can taste salt, you've added too much. Another tip is to cook your salt in; whenever you add an ingredient to the pan add a small pinch of salt along with it, building up the seasoning as you go. Salt added at the end of cooking will always be more pronounced as a flavour in a dish. It is also important to remember that, when seasoning something hot that will be served cold, you need more seasoning the colder it will be. For example, pâté needs to taste slightly over-seasoned while hot to be correctly seasoned when served cold. It is worth noting that sugar works in the same way; it seasons dishes following the same rules. When we speak of savoury food and desserts we are merely differentiating between foods seasoned with salt or sugar.

In this book I have generally given an accurate weight of salt for each recipe. This is to ensure that those unsure in the craft of seasoning have a clear guide as to how much salt is correct. Those confident with their seasoning can add salt to their own taste, but if the dish doesn't taste as delicious as you think it should, it's probably because you haven't added enough. The quantities given are for Maldon sea salt, a flaked sea salt from the UK. Every salt brings its own character and mineral balance to a dish and Maldon has the distinction of being widely available, very clean and drawing out the top notes in food very well. Feel free to use another flaked sea salt, but be aware that those with a high mineral content, such as fleur de sel, may take less salt before you begin to taste it. If you are adding salt to water for blanching then fine sea salt is adequate and cost-effective when using large quantities.

adding cayenne pepper

I use a lot more cayenne pepper than I do black pepper. This is not to say that black pepper does not have a place, it is a wonderful flavour, but I find cayenne pepper cleaner and more precise. When adding cayenne pepper to a dish you are not looking to add a flavour or even taste the pepper, you are using the pepper to lengthen the flavour of the other ingredients in the mouth. This makes the experience of the item seasoned with cayenne linger longer on the palette and take a more pronounced place in the dish.

umami

Umami is the taste in food that makes you go "Mmm, I'll have some more of that". We call it moreish, depth of flavour, savoury and even "yum". It is very in vogue to talk about umami in plant-based cookery, but you need a little bit of understanding to really get the most from it.

Umami is created by three separate chemicals:

Glutamate: This is found in plant and dairy products. It is most prevalent in fermented foods (it is the "yum factor" in sauerkraut and cheese) and slow-cooked foods such as slow-baked onions. Some of the highest plant-based sources of glutamate are soy sauce, kombu, miso, sauerkraut, sweet potatoes and onions.

Guanylate: This is found in its highest concentrations in mushrooms, especially dried mushrooms. Shiitake, morels and porcinis top the list, while nori is the only non-mushroom or meat ingredient in the top ten.

Inosinate: This is found exclusively in meat products, so is of little use to us here.

Using foods high in any one of these will greatly enhance the yummy savouriness of a food stuff. The real magic happens when you combine two of these elements together in a dish. They enhance the flavour by a degree many, many times that of just one on its own. In the perfect mushroom risotto (see page 149) I have combined massive amounts of guanylate from the dried mushrooms and other mushrooms, with glutamate from the shallots, garlic and mirepoix (see page 65). If you really wanted to give it a kick, you could use some soy sauce in place of the salt, but I am fundamentally against these umami short cuts. If you look at a lot of plant-based recipes they add soy sauce, yeast powder or miso to food stuffs that have no need of these flavours. You can get the umami from plants through solid cooking techniques and taking your time – you don't need to add it where it isn't naturally found. Step away from the soy sauce when making a tomato sauce and figure out how to enhance the depth of flavour naturally by the long, slow cooking of the tomatoes.

texture in food

When we think of a great meal we often think of how it tasted or how it looked, but we rarely think of its texture. Texture is often key to how much we enjoy a dish and, if it is done well, no one even notices. The important thing is to have a variety of textures on the plate and to have them separated so that each mouthful is subtly different: one creamy and smooth, one firm, and one crunchy. This helps to keep us interested when eating a big plate of food. A bowl of risotto tastes great, but a whole bowl of it can be a challenge. However, put some chunky vegetables in and a scattering of crunchy nuts over the top and you can eat the whole thing and still want more.

the colour of food

After flavour and texture, colour is probably my next priority when creating a dish. It is so important that the colours are clean and vibrant. It is also important that a dish with a colour in its name shows that colour clearly. Green lentils are wonderful. They have a hearty, earthy flavour, but, once cooked, they're not green, and if you blend them they go grey. The problem is that you will need to call the dish "green" lentils so people know what it contains, and then people will be expecting green on the plate. I add herbs and spinach to the green lentil & onion pâté (see page 74) to ensure that the green colour is evident, and I choose my flavours wisely to support the plainer, northern European style I am working with. In much the same way I add turmeric or saffron to yellow split peas, so they remain yellow.

equipment

All you need to cook great food is a sharp knife and somewhere to get things hot. You can produce wonderful things with a camping stove and pen knife provided the ingredients are good. That said, this book is full of modern recipes that make liberal use of specialist kitchen equipment. Below is a summary of the items I would consider key in a modern plant-based kitchen, but check the recipe before you begin, to make sure you have everything you need.

Knives

It is not worth buying expensive knives if you cannot sharpen them properly. Whet stones are the gold standard for sharpening knives, and it is worth taking the time to learn how to use one properly – there are many excellent videos available online. As a rule of thumb, you should spend as much money on your sharpening stone as you do on your knife. Good knives take a finer edge and stay sharp for longer, but all knives are the same after a month if you don't sharpen them. You are better off with a discount store knife that you sharpen well and regularly than a hand-made Japanese santoku you have never sharpened.

High-power blender

I use a blender a lot, and nearly every recipe in this book requires one. Buy a good blender with a high-power motor, basically a jet engine with a blade attached. Look for brands that emphasize smoothie making as these tend to have a bit more punch to them. Ones that come with a stick or paddle to stir while blending are often a good bet as well. The better your blender, the smoother and more refined your food will be, it's as simple as that.

Scales

A good set of electronic scales that measure down to 1g is important. Volume measurements such as litres and cups are not accurate enough for really fine cookery. A second set of small scales that weigh down as far as 0.01g are also key for modern ingredients such as xanthan gum and agar. There is no need to buy expensive ones, the most important thing is that they can weigh up to 2.5kg (5½lb) and down to 1g.

Mandolin

There are lots of expensive mandolins on the market, but I like the cheap, plastic Japanese ones as they are easy to use, sharp as a razor and easy to sharpen.

Pestle and mortar

A heavy granite mortar is ideal, but avoid those made of black granite for things like aioli, because they will turn it grey.

Pots and pans

Heavy-based saucepans will make cooking easier by holding a more stable temperature, but as long as it doesn't leak, a skilled cook can use any saucepan to make great food.

Ice-cream maker

If you're going to make a lot of the recipes from the desserts chapter (see page 187) then you will want an ice-cream maker. Those that have a built-in freezing system will produce better textures, but a cheap, pre-freeze model is better than no machine at all.

Dehydrator

This is a luxury, but it means you can be drying things out while using your oven for other purposes. Look for front-loading, tray-style machines rather than the round stacked ones.

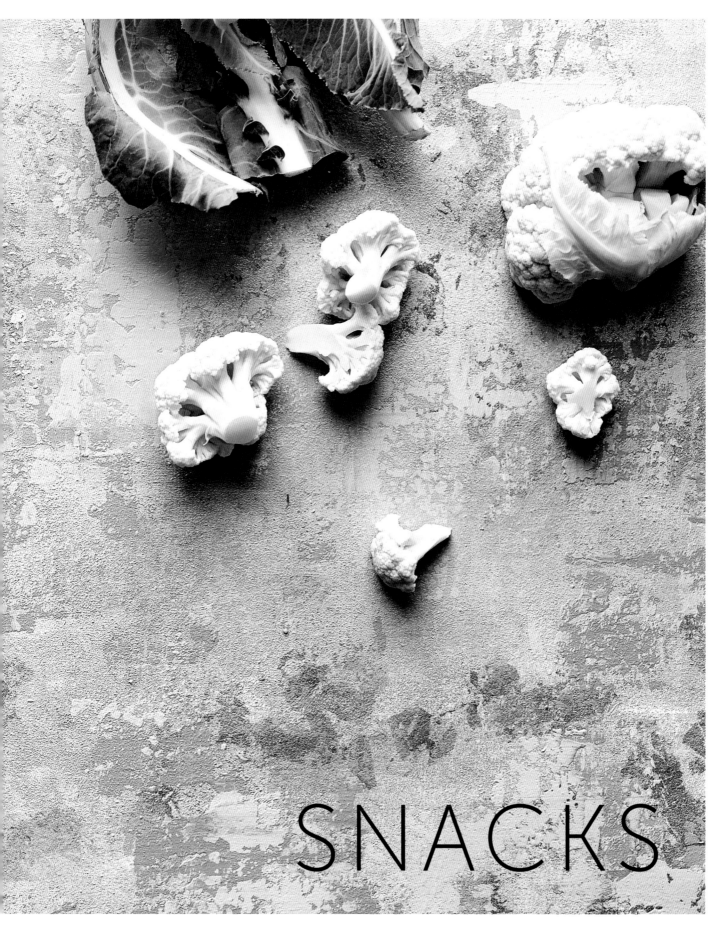

SNACKS

These nuts and seeds bring a salty depth of flavour and crunchy texture to any plate of food, or make a simple moreish snack when hunger strikes. Obviously you need to pair them well – a lovely Spanish-inspired salad doesn't sit well with the Eastern-tinged tamari flavours. The main challenge is not eating them all as soon as you make them.

Makes: 1 small jar of each

TAMARI SEEDS

20g (¾oz/⅛ cup) pumpkin seeds
40g (1½oz/⅓ cup) sunflower seeds
10g (¼oz/1¼ tbsp) poppy seeds
10g (¼oz/4 tsp) sesame seeds
1g (½ tsp) coriander seeds
1g (½ tsp) fennel seeds
25ml (1fl oz/5 tsp) tamari (or dark soy sauce such as shoyu)

Preheat the oven to (fan) 160°C/180°C/350°F/gas mark 4. Mix all the seeds together on a baking tray (sheet), spread out evenly and roast for 5 minutes until just golden. Transfer to a bowl, add the tamari and stir to evenly coat.

Return the coated seeds to the baking tray (sheet) and spread them out evenly. Bake for 4 minutes, then stir and spread out again. Bake for a further 4 minutes, then check – you want the tamari to look dry. If it is still wet, then stir and return to the oven in 2-minute bursts until dry.

Move the seeds around the baking tray (sheet) to stop them sticking and then leave until cold and crisp. The seeds will keep in an airtight jar for up to 3 months.

TAMARI CASHEWS

200g (7oz/1½ cups) cashew nuts
80ml (3fl oz/⅓ cup) tamari (or dark soy sauce such as shoyu)

Put the cashew nuts on a baking tray (sheet) then follow the recipe for Tamari Seeds (above). These will keep in an airtight jar for up to 3 months.

FRIED SPANISH ALMONDS

200g (7oz/1½ cups) whole almonds (with skin on)
50ml (2fl oz/scant ¼ cup) extra virgin olive oil
sea salt

Put the almonds into a small heatproof bowl. Pour over boiling water to cover and leave until cool. Drain the almonds and pop them from their skins.

Gently heat the olive oil in a small frying pan (skillet). Add the peeled almonds and fry gently until a light golden brown, stirring and tossing them often. Drain the almonds through a sieve set over a bowl and discard the oil. Transfer the cooked almonds to a bowl lined with kitchen (paper) towel, liberally sprinkle with salt and leave to drain. These will keep in an airtight jar for up to 2 weeks.

These fritters are delicious and nutritious. They are not subtle, however, so I wouldn't serve them with a delicate fine dining meal, but they do make a great snack, light starter or tapas on a summer's day.

Serves: 4

ALMOND & PAPRIKA FRITTERS

FOR THE FILLING

3g (1½ tsp) cumin seeds

6g (⅛oz/2½ tsp) mild smoked paprika

2g (generous ½ tsp) agar powder

3g (½ tsp) sea salt

150g (5½oz/1 cup) blanched almonds

25ml (1fl oz/5 tsp) extra virgin olive oil

150g (5½oz) diced onions

4 cloves of garlic, puréed (see page 147)

200ml (7fl oz/generous ¾ cup) water

0.75g (scant ½ tsp) cayenne pepper

7g (¼oz/2 tbsp) parsley leaves, chopped

4g (4¾ tsp) chopped tarragon leaves

FOR THE BATTER

80g (2¾oz/¾ cup) gram flour, plus extra to coat

20g (¾oz/2½ tbsp) cornflour (cornstarch)

1g (scant ¼ tsp) sea salt

4g (1¾ tsp) paprika

1g (¼ tsp) baking powder

160ml (5½fl oz/⅔ cup) cold water

vegetable oil, for deep-fat frying

TO SERVE

aioli (see page 38)

tomato chutney (see page 40)

Page 23: almond & paprika fritters with aioli. Page 24: Spanish fried cauliflower (top) and tempura kale (bottom) with tomato chutney.

Preheat the oven to (fan) 160°C/180°C/350°F/gas mark 4.

Toast the cumin seeds in a frying pan (skillet) over a medium heat until fragrant, then, using a pestle and mortar, grind to a powder. Add the paprika, agar and salt and set aside. Put the almonds on a baking tray (sheet) and toast in the oven for 7 minutes until golden.

Heat the olive oil in a frying pan (skillet), add the onion and fry until just beginning to soften. Add the garlic and cook until the onions are soft and translucent. Add the cumin and paprika mix to the onions, stir to combine, then add the measured water and bring to the boil.

Remove from the heat and transfer to a food processor. Add the almonds and process to a coarse paste. Fold through the cayenne pepper and chopped herbs and pour the mix into a bowl. Cover the top with cling film (plastic wrap) in contact with the mix to prevent a skin forming and put into the fridge for at least 30 minutes to set.

Make the aioli (see page 38) and tomato chutney (see page 40).

Once the fritter mix is set, take it out of the fridge and stir. Form into balls a little smaller than a ping pong ball and place on a plate.

Make the batter. Sieve all the dry ingredients together into a bowl, add the cold water and whisk to form a batter. Put some extra gram flour in a shallow bowl. Prepare your deep-fat fryer (see below).

Put the shaped fritters first into the dry gram flour to coat them and then, using a fork, dip them into the batter mix and then drop them into the hot oil, cooking a few at a time until they float to the surface and are golden brown. If using a deep-fat fryer, shake the basket so they don't stick. If using a saucepan, use a wooden spoon to prevent them sticking to the bottom. You may need to flip them over, using a spoon, to ensure they are evenly cooked. Once cooked remove and drain on kitchen (paper) towel, then serve hot with aioli and tomato chutney.

PREPARING YOUR DEEP-FAT FRYER

Fill a medium saucepan two-thirds full of a neutral vegetable oil or fill a deep-fat fryer with vegetable oil following the manufacturer's instructions. Heat the oil to 190°C/375°F (or slightly lower if you want a slightly slower cooking time). Place a baking tray (sheet) lined with kitchen (paper) towel next to the fryer and have a slotted spoon to hand.

If you are making the almond & paprika fritters (see opposite), it is worth making the Spanish fried cauliflower at the same time as they go very well together. You can use the fritter batter for the cauliflower if you wish. The tempura kale has a light, crispy batter and is one of the simplest, tastiest ways to cook kale that I know of.

Each serves: 4

SPANISH FRIED CAULIFLOWER

FOR THE CAULIFLOWER
1 large cauliflower, cut into
    large florets
5g (⅛ oz/2½ tsp) cumin seeds
5g (⅛ oz/2¼ tsp) smoked paprika
25g (1oz/3½ tbsp) gram flour
vegetable oil, for deep-fat frying

FOR THE BATTER
100g (3½oz/scant 1 cup) gram flour
75g (2¾oz/½ cup) potato flour
3g (½ tsp) sea salt, finely ground
10g (¼oz/4½ tsp) paprika
350ml (12fl oz/1½ cups) cold water

TO SERVE
aioli (see page 38)
tomato chutney (see page 40)

Bring a large saucepan with 4 litres (7 pints/16 cups) of water and 60g (2oz/ scant ¼ cup) of salt to the boil, then add the cauliflower florets. Cook for 3–4 minutes until soft but still al dente then shock in ice-cold water (see page 185). Dry the cauliflower florets, then put into a large bowl. Make the aioli (see page 38) and tomato chutney (see page 40).

Prepare the batter. Sieve the dry ingredients together into a bowl, then add the cold water and whisk to form a batter. Prepare your deep-fat fryer (see opposite).

Grind the cumin seeds to a powder using a pestle and mortar. Add the smoked paprika and gram flour and mix together. Sprinkle over the cauliflower and gently mix so the florets are all covered.

Put the cauliflower into the batter mix and then drop it into the hot oil. If using a deep-fat fryer, shake the basket so the cauliflower doesn't stick. If using a saucepan, use a wooden spoon to prevent it sticking to the bottom. Cook for 2–3 minutes until golden, then drain on kitchen (paper) towel. Repeat with all the cauliflower florets and serve with some fiery aioli.

TEMPURA KALE

FOR THE TEMPURA KALE
20 small, tender kale leaves
300g (10½oz/scant 2½ cups) plain
    (all-purpose) flour
20g (¾oz/2½ tbsp) cornflour
    (cornstarch)
2g (⅓ tsp) sea salt
5g (⅛oz/1 tsp) baking powder
300ml (10fl oz/1¼ cups) cold water
vegetable oil, for deep-fat frying

TO SERVE
aioli (see page 38)

Make the aioli (see page 38). Wash the kale leaves and dry thoroughly.

Make the tempura batter by sieving together 200g (7oz/1⅔ cups) of the flour with the cornflour (cornstarch), salt and baking powder. Add the cold water and stir loosely to combine with a fork, but do not overstir or your batter will be tough. Prepare your deep-fat fryer (see opposite).

Toss a kale leaf in the remaining flour, dip it into the tempura batter and drop it into the deep-fat fryer. If using a deep-fat fryer, shake the basket so the kale doesn't stick. If using a saucepan, use a wooden spoon to prevent it sticking to the bottom. Once the batter is golden, remove and drain on kitchen (paper) towel. Repeat for all the kale leaves, cooking them one at a time, and serve with aioli.

| CRISPS |

SWEET POTATO CRISPS

This is a great way to make crisps to add a bit of crunch to a plate. It takes some practice, but it carries more vegetable flavour than deep-frying and keeps a better shape.

Makes: 8 crisps

1 large sweet potato, peeled and cut in half lengthways
1g (scant ¼ tsp) sea salt
4g (1 tsp) caster (superfine) sugar

Preheat the oven to (fan) 140°C/160°C/310°F/gas mark 2½.

Slice the sweet potato finely using a mandolin. Choose 8 of the best slices and place in a bowl. Sprinkle with the salt and sugar and leave for 20 minutes to soften.

Pat the sweet potato slices dry with kitchen (paper) towel and spread them out on a large baking tray (sheet) lined with non-stick baking parchment. Cover with another sheet of baking parchment, pressing down with another slightly smaller tray to make sure the crisps are flat.

Bake the crisps for 7 minutes, then check. If they are starting to crisp, remove the extra baking tray (sheet) and return to the oven for 4-minute bursts until crisp but not coloured. Remove the top sheet of baking parchment and, if needed, return to the oven for 2 minutes maximum to dry out.

Allow the crisps to cool – they should become crispier and brittle as they cool. If they are still a bit wet return them to the oven in short bursts until ready.

These will keep for up to 3 days in an airtight container.

SPRING GREEN CRISPS

A quick, easy-to-make crisp that adds drama, texture and nuttiness to any plate.

Makes: 8–10 crisps

4 large, dark, spring green leaves
extra virgin olive oil, to drizzle
sea salt, to sprinkle

Preheat the oven to (fan) 140°C/160°C/310°F/gas mark 2½.

Trim the spring green leaves, remove and discard the stalk, then cut the leaves into shards approximately 10 x 4cm (4 x 1½ inches). Put the leaves in a small bowl and toss them in a little oil and salt, then spread flat on a large baking tray (sheet) so they are not touching each other.

Bake for 7 minutes, then check. They should look crisp and dry around the edges with no soggy patches, but not burnt on the edges. If they have not reached this point then return them to the oven in 3-minute bursts until ready. Remove from the oven and allow them to cool and go crisp.

These will keep for up to 3 days in an airtight container.

CAVOLO NERO CRISPS

A simple variation of the spring green crisps (see above), but, as cavolo nero is a thicker leaf, you just need to pay a little more attention to check that it has dried fully and isn't still soggy in places.

Makes: 8 crisps

8 cavolo nero leaves
extra virgin olive oil, to drizzle
sea salt, to sprinkle

Preheat the oven to (fan) 160°C/180°C/350°F/gas mark 4. If using large cavolo nero leaves, remove the stem from each leaf and trim the edges if necessary. Toss in a little oil and salt and lay on a baking tray (sheet). Bake in the oven for 10–15 minutes until dry and crisp but not coloured, then leave to cool and crisp up.

These will keep in an airtight container for 3 days.

Hummus is that great vegetarian classic that has become synonymous with plant-based eating, sadly often in a derogatory way. One reason is there are so many recipes that are grainy, bland and uninspiring. Correctly made, hummus is decadent, moreish and elegant. For me, the perfect hummus has a creamy, smooth texture that disappears in the mouth. The trick to achieving this is by peeling the chickpeas (garbanzo beans) and adding enough oil. It may seem like a pain, but peeling your chickpeas (garbanzo beans) will make the difference between a melting, creamy texture and something that is just okay.

Serves: 4

PERFECT HUMMUS

80–100g (2¾–3½oz) dried chickpeas (garbanzo beans) or 400g (14oz) canned (240g/8½oz drained weight)

2g (½ tsp) bicarbonate of soda (baking soda) (if using dried beans)

2g (1 tsp) cumin seeds

2 cloves of garlic, peeled but whole

25ml (1fl oz/5 tsp) lemon juice

40g (1½oz/scant 3 tbsp) tahini

100ml (3½fl oz/scant ½ cup) extra virgin olive oil, plus extra to drizzle

70ml (2½fl oz/generous ¼ cup) cold water

4g (¾ tsp) sea salt

TO SERVE

harissa dressing (see page 41)

zaalouk (see opposite)

flat breads (see page 217)

If using dried chickpeas (garbanzo beans), put them in a bowl and cover with cold water by at least 4cm (1½ inches). Leave for at least 8 hours or ideally overnight.

Make the harissa dressing (see page 41), zaalouk (see opposite) and flat breads (see page 217).

Drain and rinse the dried chickpeas (garbanzo beans) and place in a small lidded saucepan with 1 litre (1¾ pints/4 cups) of cold water and the bicarbonate of soda (baking soda). Bring to the boil and simmer gently for 40–50 minutes, adding more water if it begins to run dry, until the chickpeas (garbanzo beans) are very soft with no grainy texture. When cooked, drain and rinse the chickpeas (garbanzo beans) and put them into a large bowl. Or drain and rinse the canned chickpeas (garbanzo beans), reserving the liquid for aquafaba (see page 76). Rub the chickpeas (garbanzo beans) vigorously between the palms of your hands until the skins come loose (don't worry if they break up a bit). Cover with cold water and agitate them until all the skins float to the surface, removing them as you go. Drain and discard the water and put the peeled chickpeas (garbanzo beans) into a blender.

Put the cumin seeds into a small frying pan (skillet) and heat gently until fragrant but not burnt. Grind to a fine powder using a pestle and mortar and add to the chickpeas (garbanzo beans) along with the rest of the ingredients. Blend for up to 5 minutes, until completely smooth, adding a little more water if necessary. Check the seasoning (see page 15), add more salt if needed, then chill in the fridge for at least 2 hours.

Swirl the hummus into a bowl, add a generous drizzle of olive oil and top with the harissa dressing. Serve with flat breads and zaalouk.

DRIED VERSUS CANNED BEANS

There is always the debate when making something from legumes as to whether it is better to use dried or canned. The feeling is that soaking and cooking dried beans is "proper cooking", and canned beans are a bit of a cheat. There is some truth in this, and it does give you more control over the cooking process; however, dried beans are a seasonal product and should be young and fresh, preferably less than a year old. Old beans have a floury texture, take hours to cook and have no flavour beside that of dried beans. If you can find out how old the beans are, use dried, but if you can't, use the best-quality canned or jarred beans that you can get.

This recipe is a relatively new discovery for me. Until I found this traditional Moroccan recipe the short English aubergine (eggplant) season meant I made babaganoush, which, while delicious, is tainted by hemp shirts and sandals. I think that zaalouk is much more delicious than babaganoush, and it also makes great use of the tomatoes that are ripe at exactly the same time. It always tastes better after a night in the fridge so, if you have time, try to make it at least a day ahead of eating.

Serves: 4

ZAALOUK

1 large aubergine (eggplant) (about 500g/1lb 2oz)
7g (¼oz/3½ tsp) cumin seeds
7g (¼oz/1¼ tsp) sea salt
7g (¼oz/1 tbsp) smoked paprika
4 large plum tomatoes
4 cloves of garlic, puréed (see page 147)
15g (½oz/¼ cup) parsley leaves, finely chopped, plus extra to garnish
30ml (1fl oz/2 tbsp) extra virgin olive oil
75ml (2¾fl oz/⅓ cup) water
10ml (2 tsp) lemon juice
2g (1 tsp) ground black pepper

TO SERVE
harissa dressing (see page 41)
perfect hummus (see opposite)
flat breads (see page 217)
extra virgin olive oil, to drizzle
black pepper

Preheat the oven to (fan) 160°C/180°C/350°F/gas mark 4.

Spike the aubergine (eggplant) with a fork or sharp knife 2 or 3 times and place on a small baking tray (sheet). Roast in the oven for 30 minutes until soft, then leave to cool before cutting in half lengthways. Scoop out the flesh and discard the skin. Cut the flesh into rough dice, each about 1.5cm (½ inch), and transfer to a large frying pan (skillet).

Put the cumin seeds into a small frying pan (skillet) and toast over a medium heat until you can just begin to smell them. Transfer to a pestle and mortar and grind to a powder. Add the salt and smoked paprika, stir, then add to the aubergine (eggplant).

Remove the stem from the tomatoes and cut into 1.5cm (½-inch) dice. Add the tomatoes, garlic, parsley, olive oil and water to the frying pan (skillet) containing the aubergine (eggplant) and bring to a gentle simmer. Cook gently for 30 minutes, stirring often, adding an occasional splash of water if necessary. When ready, the mix should be thick and rich. Add the lemon juice and black pepper and stir to combine.

Transfer to a container, leave to cool, then place in the fridge for at least a few hours and ideally overnight.

Make the harissa dressing (see page 41), perfect hummus (see opposite) and flat breads (see page 217).

When ready to eat, transfer the zaalouk to a serving bowl and add a drizzle of olive oil and a twist of black pepper. Serve with harissa dressing, hummus and flat breads.

I'm a big fan of gram flour: it has a great flavour, is gluten-free and highly nutritious. The trick is to remember to make your batter ahead of time to allow it to ferment overnight. This removes any raw bean flavour and adds a sour nuttiness that is unique to gram flour. You can make this with or without the garlic – it will still work really well without it.

Serves: 4–8

GARLIC PANISSE

250g (9oz/2¼ cups) gram flour

50g (1¾oz/scant ⅓ cup) polenta (cornmeal)

1 litre (1¾ pints/4 cups) water

12 cloves of garlic

200ml (7fl oz/generous ¾ cup) extra virgin olive oil

8g (¼ oz/1½ tsp) sea salt

vegetable oil, for deep-fat frying

TO SERVE

tomato chutney (see page 40)

You need to make the panisse batter a day in advance. In a bowl, whisk the gram flour, polenta and water together. Leave in a warm place (22°C/71°F) for 24 hours.

Preheat the oven to (fan) 100°C/120°C/240°F/gas mark ¼–½. Place the garlic cloves in a small ovenproof dish and cover completely with the olive oil. Bake in the oven for 30–40 minutes until very soft but not coloured, then allow to cool. (The garlic and oil will keep in the fridge for 3 months.) Make the tomato chutney (see page 40).

Remove the garlic from the oil and grind to a fine paste using a pestle and mortar. Put the panisse batter into a saucepan and add the salt and garlic paste. Whisk to make sure it is smooth, then gently heat, stirring all the time using a silicon spatula. As it approaches the boil it will thicken dramatically – keep stirring until the spatula stands up in the mix.

Pour the mix onto a board or tray lined with non-stick baking parchment. Spread to a 1.5cm (½-inch) thickness. Lay another sheet of baking parchment on top and press down slightly. Leave to cool to room temperature, then transfer to the fridge and chill for 1 hour.

Prepare your deep-fat fryer (see page 26). Cut the chilled panisse into 1.5cm (½-inch) strips, then cut these strips into chips about 3–5cm (1¼–2 inches) long. Deep-fry (see page 26) the panisse in batches for about 2 minutes, then drain on kitchen (paper) towel. Serve hot with tomato chutney.

These polenta chips are a delicious alternative to potato chips and have a fantastic crunchy outer and creamy inner. The rosemary adds a nice herbal note but can be switched for other savoury herbs or even green olives.

The rosti are so simple and delicious it seems a shame to mess with them, but you can add herbs, especially sage or thyme should you wish. Serve either the rosti or polenta chips as part of a plant-based fried breakfast and you will have friends for life.

Each serves: 4

ROSEMARY POLENTA CHIPS

1.1 litres (2 pints/4½ cups) basic
   stock (see page 64)
225g (8oz/1⅓ cups) polenta
   (cornmeal), plus extra to dust
5g (⅛oz/3 tbsp) rosemary, finely
   chopped
40ml (1½fl oz/8 tsp) extra virgin
   olive oil
5g (⅛oz/1 tsp) sea salt
vegetable oil, for deep-fat frying

TO SERVE
aioli (see page 38)
tomato chutney (see page 40)

Make the aioli (see page 38) and tomato chutney (see page 40).

Put the stock into a saucepan and bring to the boil. Sprinkle in the polenta (cornmeal), whisk with a wire whisk until it begins to thicken, then stir continuously with a wooden spoon or silicon spatula. When it is thick enough that the wooden spoon stands up in it, add the rosemary, olive oil and salt and stir well to combine.

Pour onto a large board lined with non-stick baking parchment and spread out into a rectangle 1cm (½ inch) thick. Allow to cool completely, then cut into 1cm (½-inch) strips. Cut these into chip shapes and dust with polenta (cornmeal). Prepare your deep-fat fryer (see page 26).

Deep-fry (see page 26) or shallow-fry the chips in batches (they will take 2–4 minutes), then drain on kitchen (paper) towel. Serve hot with tomato chutney and aioli.

ROSTI

900g (2lb) floury potatoes, such as
   rooster or maris piper
100g (3½oz) finely sliced onions
10g (¼oz/1¾ tsp) sea salt
30g (1¼oz/4 tbsp) gram flour
rapeseed oil, to fry

TO SERVE
aioli (see page 38)
tomato chutney (see page 40)

Wash but don't peel the potatoes, then coarsely grate into a large bowl and add the onion and salt. Massage with your fingers, then transfer to a colander over a large bowl and leave to drain for 1 hour, occasionally pressing the mix down and mixing it around.

Make the aioli (see page 38) and tomato chutney (see page 40).

After 1 hour remove the potato mix and squeeze to remove as much liquid as possible. Transfer the mix to a clean bowl and loosen with your fingers. Sieve the gram flour over and mix with your fingers so the potato is evenly covered.

Preheat the oven to its lowest setting. Take 1 tablespoon of the mix and form into a flat fritter shape about 7mm (⅓ inch) thick. Lay out on a tray and repeat with the rest of the mix. Cover the base of a large frying pan (skillet) with about 5mm (¼ inch) of rapeseed oil and heat to 180°C/350°F. Add the rosti in batches and fry until golden and crisp on one side, then turn over. Fry until golden on the other side, then place on a lined baking tray (sheet) and keep warm in the oven while you cook the rest, topping up with more oil if necessary. Serve hot with tomato chutney and aioli.

| ACCOMPANIMENTS |

AIOLI

True aioli is a thing of beauty, incredibly garlicky and very hard to make. This version is technically a garlic mayonnaise but is foolproof to make and I think tastes more palatable than its fearsome namesake. Use the oil you prefer, bearing in mind that olive oil will be very strongly flavoured.

Makes: 300ml (10fl oz) jar

50ml (2fl oz/scant ¼ cup) aquafaba (see page 76)
1–2 cloves of garlic
20ml (¾fl oz/4 tsp) cider vinegar or 25ml (1fl oz/5 tsp) lemon juice
2g (⅓ tsp) sea salt
150ml (5fl oz/⅔ cup) oil (see above)

Put the aquafaba, garlic, cider vinegar (or lemon juice) and salt into a blender and blend until smooth. Transfer the oil to a jug or container you can pour slowly from.

Set your blender onto a medium speed and very slowly add the oil, a small splash at a time until about half of it has gone into creating a smooth, glossy, emulsified liquid. Speed up the pouring and as you near the end the mix will miraculously turn into a thick glossy mayonnaise and you will be unable to blend any more. This will keep in a jar in the fridge for up to a month.

BLACK OLIVE TAPENADE

I use this as a salty foil for the sweet tomatoes in the confit tomato salad (see page 106), but it is a great thing to have to hand and eat with bread and wine when the mood takes you. For an extra-special version use half extra virgin olive oil and half black truffle oil.

Makes: 250ml (8½fl oz) jar

200g (7oz/1¼ cups) pitted kalamata olives, rinsed and drained
20g (¾oz/⅛ cup) capers, rinsed and drained
15ml (1 tbsp) red wine vinegar
50ml (2fl oz/scant ¼ cup) extra virgin olive oil (or see above)

Put all the ingredients into a food processor and process to make a paste. This will keep in the fridge for at least 2 weeks.

FIG CHUTNEY

Just typing this recipe is making my mouth water. This is my favourite chutney in the world and is a great way to add sweet and sour depth to any salad or lunch.

Makes: 500ml (18fl oz) jar

250g (9oz/1⅔ cups) dried figs
1 onion, diced
1 Bramley apple, peeled, cored and diced
20g (¾oz) organic ginger (see page 60), grated
finely grated zest of 1 lemon
125ml (4fl oz/½ cup) cider vinegar
100g (3½oz/generous ½ cup) soft brown sugar
5g (⅛ oz/2½ tsp) mild Madras curry powder
1g (⅔ tsp) chilli flakes (crushed chilli)
4g (¾ tsp) sea salt
300ml (10fl oz/1¼ cups) water

Remove and discard the stalks from the figs and cut each fig into 8 pieces. Put all the ingredients into a small saucepan and simmer gently for up to an hour until everything has completely broken down. Leave to cool, then store in a sealed jar or container. This will keep in a jar in the fridge for at least 3 months.

« mustard

« fig chutney

« aioli

tomato chutney »

pesto »

TOMATO CHUTNEY

Some recipes, like the garlic panisse (see page 36), or rosemary polenta chips (see page 37), while delicious on their own, are really just vehicles for a good sauce or chutney. If that is the case then this is the chutney you need. It's not clever, but it is very, very tasty. Make a lot as it will keep for ages in the fridge, and you can eat it with anything that comes out of your deep-fat fryer.

Makes: 500ml (18fl oz) jar

3g (1½ tsp) cumin seeds
5g (⅛ oz/2 tsp) smoked paprika
5g (⅛ oz/1 tsp) sea salt
25ml (1fl oz/5 tsp) extra virgin olive oil
1 banana shallot, finely diced
1 red chilli, halved, deseeded, finely chopped
10g (¼oz) organic ginger (see page 60), finely grated
1 clove of garlic, puréed (see page 147)
3g (1½ tsp) fennel seeds
400g (14oz) can of plum tomatoes
150g (5½oz/generous ¾ cup) soft brown sugar
75ml (2¾fl oz/⅓ cup) red wine vinegar

Fry the cumin seeds in a small frying pan (skillet) until fragrant, then grind to a fine powder using a pestle and mortar. Add the smoked paprika and salt and mix.

Gently heat the olive oil in a saucepan. Add the shallot and cook for 1 minute, then add the chilli, ginger and garlic and fry briefly. Add the fennel seeds and paprika/cumin mix and then add the tomatoes. Cook until the tomatoes are broken down and thick, then add the sugar and vinegar. Cook until thick and glossy. Remove from the heat and leave to cool.

This will keep in a jar in the fridge for up to 3 months.

PESTO

As with most things made with raw garlic, this will taste better if left to mellow overnight. Use the best-quality basil you can find – this is a basil sauce after all!

Makes: 500ml (18fl oz) jar

100g (3½oz/¾ cup) pine nuts
2 cloves of garlic, chopped
2g (⅓ tsp) sea salt
150g (5½oz/6 cups) basil leaves, roughly chopped
250ml (8½fl oz/1 cup) extra virgin olive oil
50ml (2fl oz/scant ¼ cup) lemon juice

Preheat the oven to (fan) 160°C/180°C/350°F/gas mark 4. Put the pine nuts onto a small baking tray (sheet) and roast in the oven for 7 minutes until just golden brown. Set aside to cool.

If making by hand, grind the garlic and salt to a paste using a large pestle and mortar. Add the pine nuts and smash to a coarse crumb. Add the basil a little at a time, grinding it to a paste before adding the next batch. If it starts to get too thick, add a little oil to loosen. Once all the basil is incorporated, add any remaining oil and the lemon juice.

If making in a food processor, process the garlic, salt and pine nuts to a coarse lumpy crumb. Add the basil, oil and lemon juice and process to a coarse purée.

Taste and adjust the seasoning as necessary (see page 15). This will keep in a jar in the fridge for up to a month.

HARISSA DRESSING

Sometimes you want a bit of kick on your plate. Serve this in place of the tomato chutney (see opposite), or with the perfect hummus (see page 32) or zaalouk (see page 33). It would even pep up the pistachio pâté (see page 66) if you like things spicy.

Makes: 250ml (8½fl oz) bottle

10 cloves of garlic, peeled but whole
10 red chillies, roughly chopped
1 small banana shallot, coarsely chopped
5g (⅛oz/2½ tsp) cumin seeds
3g (1½ tsp) coriander seeds
5g (⅛oz/2½ tsp) fennel seeds
4g (1¾ tsp) smoked paprika
125ml (4fl oz/½ cup) extra virgin olive oil
100ml (3½fl oz/scant ½ cup) water
5g (⅛oz/1 tsp) sea salt
10ml (2 tsp) red wine vinegar

Put the garlic, chillies and shallot into a blender.

Heat a small frying pan (skillet) and toast the cumin and coriander seeds for 20–30 seconds until they go a shade darker. Add to the blender along with the rest of the ingredients and blend until completely smooth.

This will keep in a jar in the fridge for at least 3 days.

MUSTARD

You can buy very good mustards nearly everywhere now, but it is very easy to make yourself and that way you can have it exactly as you like it. In my experience, this gets better and better the older it is: three weeks is the minimum time to mature, and it is really good after six months.

Makes: 500ml (18fl oz) jar

175g (6¼oz/generous 1 cup) yellow mustard seeds
50g (1¾oz/⅓ cup) brown mustard seeds
175ml (6fl oz/¾ cup) boiling water
225ml (7½fl oz/scant 1 cup) cider vinegar
125g (4½oz/⅔ cup) caster (superfine) sugar
15g (½oz/2¾ tsp) sea salt
4 cloves of garlic, peeled
5g (⅛oz/2 tbsp) chopped tarragon

Sterilize a 500ml (18fl oz) glass jar by bringing a large saucepan of water to the boil and submerging the jar and lid in it. Boil for 10 minutes and then carefully remove. Allow to cool and dry.

Mix the mustard seeds together and transfer 75g (2¾oz/½ cup) of the mixed seeds to a spice grinder. Grind until a flour consistency, then put into a large bowl with the remaining mustard seeds. Cover with the boiling water and stir. Leave for 10 minutes.

Meanwhile, put the cider vinegar, sugar and salt into a small saucepan and gently warm, stirring, to dissolve the sugar. As soon as the sugar is dissolved, remove from the heat and allow to cool slightly.

Bring a small saucepan of water to the boil and cook the peeled garlic for 3 minutes. Remove the garlic and crush to a fine paste (see page 147).

Once the seeds have sat for 10 minutes, add the vinegar mix, garlic and tarragon and stir to combine. Transfer to the sterile jar and seal. Leave in the fridge for at least 3 weeks to mature before using.

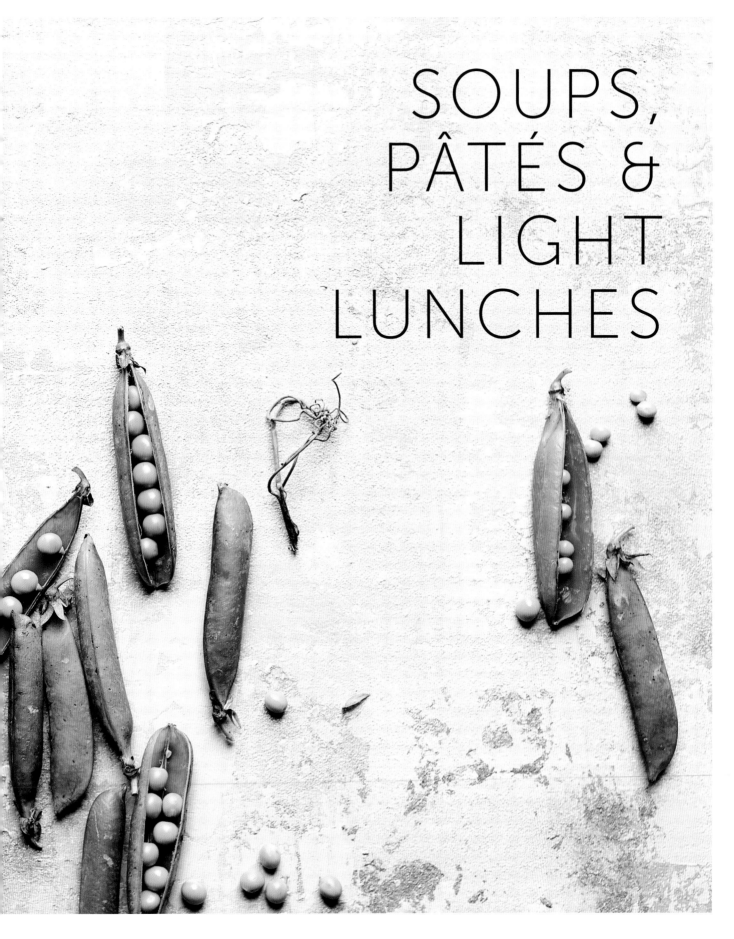

SOUPS, PÂTÉS & LIGHT LUNCHES

I live in a cottage in rural Somerset and my beautiful little garden is a never-ending source of inspiration through the balmy summer months. Looking out through the kitchen window I can see a profusion of herbs, peas and beans all clambering for space, climbing the walls and tumbling out of pots. This is an attempt to capture that feeling of verdant abundance in a little bowl of chilled soup. The combination I've used is simply what I can lay my hands on straight from the garden, so mix and match depending on what you have available and what is best in season.

Serves: 4

PEA AND HERB SOUP
with almond foam

FOR THE SOUP

25g (1oz/scant 1 cup) spinach
25g (1oz/½ cup) chives
25g (1oz/⅓ cup) parsley
2g (2 tsp) chopped tarragon
250g (9oz/1⅔ cups) freshly podded peas
50ml (2fl oz/scant ¼ cup) extra virgin olive oil
100g (3½oz) banana shallots, sliced
2.5g (1 tbsp) thyme leaves
350ml (12fl oz/1½ cups) water
sea salt

FOR THE FOAM

50g (1¾oz/⅓ cup) whole almonds
5ml (1 tsp) white wine vinegar
1 clove of garlic
200ml (7oz/generous ¾ cup) water
2g (⅓ tsp) sea salt
soy lecithin

FOR THE GARNISH

100g (3½oz) broad beans (fava beans), podded
50g (1¾oz) sugar snap peas, deveined
50g (1¾oz/⅓ cup) freshly podded peas
1 spring onion (scallion), finely sliced
4 parsley or micro parsley leaves, plus extra to top
8 lemon balm leaves
extra virgin olive oil, to drizzle
4 large radishes

First make the soup. Blanch the spinach, chives, parsley and tarragon together until the parsley is wilted and a vibrant green, then shock in ice-cold water (see page 185). Squeeze out the water using your hands, making a ball. Roughly chop and set aside. Refill the saucepan and bring to the boil. Boil the peas for a few minutes until cooked with no grainy texture, then drain and shock in ice-cold water (see page 185).

Heat the olive oil in a saucepan and add the shallots. Cook until soft and translucent, then add the thyme. Cook for 1 minute, leave to cool completely, then transfer to a blender. Add the chopped herbs, peas and measured water. Blend until very smooth, pass through a sieve and season with salt to taste (see page 15). Place in the fridge.

Next make the almond foam. Preheat the oven to (fan) 160°C/180°C/350°F/gas mark 4. Put the almonds onto a small baking tray (sheet) and roast for 10 minutes, until a dark colour. Transfer to a blender, add the vinegar, garlic, water and salt and blend until very smooth.

Line a sieve with a 30cm (12-inch) square muslin (cheesecloth) and set it over a jug. Pour the almond mix into the sieve and collect up the corners to make a bag. Twist the bag to squeeze out as much liquid as you can. Discard the almond meal in the bag and then measure the liquid. For every 100ml (3½fl oz/scant ½ cup) of liquid add 1.5g (⅔ tsp) of soy lecithin. Using a stick blender, blend the lecithin into the mix.

Next make the garnish. Blanch the broad beans (fava beans), sugar snap peas and podded peas until just soft, then shock in ice-cold water (see page 185). Dry on kitchen (paper) towel then place in a bowl, reserving a few sugar snap pea pods for garnish, add the spring onion (scallion) and shred the parsley and lemon balm over. Drizzle with a little olive oil. Place a pile of the bean and pea mix into each of 4 wide soup bowls. Finely slice the radish on a mandolin to give wafer thin slices and add to the pile along with a couple of just opened sugar snap pea pods.

Using a stick blender, whizz the almond foam at high speed, just skimming the surface of the liquid – keep whizzing until you have a beautiful, dense foam. Spoon the foam next to the pea salad and top with a few sprigs of herbs. Add the soup or pour the soup at the table from a jug for added effect.

This is a very simple soup but is brought to life by the fermented wadi and fenugreek oil. It tastes purely of cauliflower, and while that is very nice, it is designed as a backdrop for other flavours to play over and not to be eaten all on its own. Feel free to adapt this as you wish, just make sure you give it an interesting garnish and note that if using fenugreek oil, it needs to be made two weeks before using.

Serves: 4

CAULIFLOWER SOUP
with red lentil wadi

FOR THE WADI

200g (7oz/1 cup) red lentils
pinch of asafoetida
1g (¼ tsp) fenugreek powder
pinch of cayenne pepper
3g (½ tsp) sea salt
rapeseed oil, for deep-fat frying

FOR THE SOUP

1.5 litres (2½ pints/6 cups) basic
   stock (see page 64)
1kg (2¼lb) cauliflower (without the
   stem or leaves)
40ml (1½fl oz/8 tsp) rapeseed oil
1 onion, sliced
sea salt
2 cloves of garlic, puréed (see
   page 147)
50ml (2fl oz/scant ¼ cup) extra
   virgin olive oil or hazelnut oil
pinch of cayenne pepper
fenugreek oil (see page 220) or
   truffle oil

Make the fenugreek oil (see page 220) at least 2 weeks before using or use truffle oil. You need to start making the red lentil wadi a day before eating. Put the lentils in a bowl and cover with cold water by at least 2cm (¾ inch). Leave to soak for at least 6 hours or preferably overnight.

Drain the lentils and rinse well. Put into a blender with the asafoetida, fenugreek powder and cayenne pepper, and blend until a smooth paste, adding a little water if needed. The mix should be thick enough to stand on a spoon, not runny. Transfer to a sterile container (see page 101) and put in a warm place (22°C/71°F) for 8–24 hours. It should have fermented and taken on a slightly sour aroma. Mix well, stir in the salt, then place in the fridge to firm up.

Next make the soup. Make the basic stock (see page 64). Cut the cauliflower into quarters, then slice each quarter into 1cm (½-inch) slices. Put the rapeseed oil into a large saucepan and heat gently. Add the onion and a generous pinch of salt, turn down the heat and cook gently for about 20 minutes until soft but not coloured. Add the garlic and cook for 3 more minutes, then add the cauliflower and another pinch of salt and cook for 2 minutes. Add the stock, bring to the boil, then simmer gently with a lid on for about 20 minutes until the cauliflower is cooked.

Transfer the cauliflower mix to a blender and add the olive oil. Blend, in batches if necessary, until silky smooth. Pass through a sieve and season with salt and a pinch of cayenne pepper (see page 15). Return to the saucepan and keep warm.

Prepare your deep-fat fryer (see page 26). Take two-thirds of a tablespoon of the wadi mix, and, using another spoon, push it off into the hot oil. Shake the basket to prevent it sticking and add another spoonful. Once they have floated to the surface and are a golden brown colour, flip them over to make sure both sides cook evenly. Remove and drain on kitchen (paper) towel. Continue until all the mix is used.

Serve the wadi floating on top of the cauliflower soup with a drizzle of fenugreek oil over the top.

Sweetcorn is a surprisingly versatile ingredient – lightly boiled it has a sweet simplicity, but charred it is complex and delicious. Bring these two flavour profiles together and you have a balanced plate of food. Although a different variety, popcorn is another delicious way to cook corn. It is simply three nice ways of using the corn in one dish. Adding a touch of madras curry powder helps add some wonderful aromas over the sweet, charred base flavour.

Serves: 4

SWEETCORN SOUP
with charred sweetcorn and curried popcorn

FOR THE SOUP
1 litre (1¾ pints/4 cups) basic stock
  (see page 64)
25ml (1fl oz/5 tsp) rapeseed oil, plus
  extra to drizzle
1 onion, sliced
3 yellow (bell) peppers, deseeded
  and sliced
500g (1lb 2oz) sweetcorn kernels
  (fresh or frozen)
sea salt

FOR THE CHARRED SWEETCORN
1 ear of sweetcorn
extra virgin olive oil
sea salt

FOR THE GARNISH
extra virgin olive oil, to drizzle
curried popcorn (see page 117)

Make the curried popcorn (see page 117) and the basic stock (see page 64).

Heat the rapeseed oil in a large saucepan and add the onion. Cook gently until soft and translucent, then add the peppers and cook until soft. Next add the sweetcorn and stock. Cover with a lid and bring to the boil. As soon as the soup boils, check the kernels are cooked, and if soft remove from the heat. Leave the mix to cool, then process in a blender (in batches if necessary) until silky smooth. Pass through a sieve into a clean saucepan and season with salt (see page 15). Warm gently while you cook the charred sweetcorn.

Strip the leaves from the sweetcorn and remove any strings. Heat a heavy saucepan to a very high temperature. Add the sweetcorn and cook until it starts to blacken in spots. Turn slightly and repeat until the whole sweetcorn is well charred. Cut into slices and drizzle with olive oil and a generous pinch of salt.

Serve the hot soup in bowls with a good drizzle of olive oil and a scattering of curried popcorn over the top. Serve 1–2 sweetcorn pieces alongside it.

I was served a variation of this soup by my friend Silvana at the Foodie Bugle and it has stuck with me ever since. It took me over a year to summon up the courage to ask her for the recipe, and it has since become a firm summer favourite. My version omits the passata, which she insists is essential to its authenticity, but I find detracts from the freshness.

This is not a fine soup, it is rustic peasant food, made from the freshest, simplest ingredients, and is best made a day in advance for the flavours to mature. To blend it too smoothly detracts from its character. To garnish it, simply add some diced cucumber, tomato, Romano red pepper and onion and pile it on top with a load of fresh herbs, or add a drizzle of peppery olive oil. Serve it cold with crusty bread, and a fresh green salad if you wish.

Serves: 4

GAZPACHO

1 small cucumber, peeled and
    sliced
3 spring onions (scallions), coarsely
    chopped
1 red (bell) pepper, roughly
    chopped
2 cloves of garlic, peeled and
    central stem removed
15g (½oz/⅔ cup) basil
10g (¼oz/generous ⅓ cup)
    oregano
30ml (1fl oz/2 tbsp) extra virgin
    olive oil
45ml (1½fl oz/3 tbsp) red wine
    vinegar
1kg (2¼lb) ripe, juicy tomatoes
    (the best you can find)
sea salt
black pepper

FOR THE GARNISH
½ cucumber, half diced and half
    sliced and rolled
2 tomatoes, diced
1 Romano red pepper, diced
1 small onion or spring onion
    (scallion), sliced
16 small basil leaves
extra virgin olive oil

Put all the gazpacho ingredients, except the tomatoes, salt and pepper, into a blender and process slowly until semi-smooth (this is not meant to be silky smooth). Transfer to a large mixing bowl.

Quarter the tomatoes and add to the blender. Process until almost smooth, with just a bit of texture, then add to the mixing bowl along with salt and pepper to taste (see page 15). Cover and store in the fridge overnight for the flavours to come together.

Serve cold with a garnish of cucumber, tomatoes, Romano red pepper, onion and basil. Add a good glug of olive oil to each bowl and serve.

Leek and potato soup is perhaps the humblest of all meals. Two of the cheapest ingredients you can buy made into a soup, the simplest meal format imaginable. It is also a great test of a cook's skill. Leeks are a difficult vegetable to work with and are most usefully thought of as two vegetables in one. The white part is best treated as an onion, while the green part is better treated as a cabbage. Trying to emphasize the sweet, oniony depth of the leek while keeping the bright green of the top, bringing just enough of the sulphurous edge to add character without ruining the soup, can be tricky. If you don't want to make the leek and potato cakes, then simply serve the soup with a drizzle of your favourite oil.

Serves: 4

LEEK & POTATO SOUP
with leek & potato cakes

FOR THE POTATO CAKES
1 large 400g (14oz) starchy baking
   potato, washed, but skin left on
sea salt
25ml (1fl oz/5 tsp) extra virgin
   olive oil
1 leek, finely sliced
7g (¼oz/¾ tbsp) cornflour
   (cornstarch)
2g (2⅓ tsp) chopped tarragon
sunflower oil, to fry

FOR THE SOUP
800ml (28fl oz/3⅓ cups) basic
   stock (see page 64)
150g (5½oz) Jersey royal potatoes
   (or buttery textured new
   potatoes), washed but not peeled
400g (14oz) tender leeks
1 bay leaf
1 clove
60ml (2¼fl oz/¼ cup) extra virgin
   olive oil
150g (5½oz) finely sliced onion
sea salt

First make the leek and potato cakes. Chop the potato into 2cm (¾-inch) cubes. Put into a small saucepan, cover with cold water and add ½ teaspoon of salt. Bring to the boil and simmer gently until the potatoes are soft. Heat the olive oil in a small frying pan (skillet) and add the sliced leek. Sweat the leeks until soft and sweet but not coloured.

Drain the potatoes and mash until smooth. Mix in the cornflour (cornstarch), leek and tarragon. Check for seasoning and add salt if needed (see page 15). Spread the mix out onto a work surface and use a 2cm (¾-inch) cookie cutter to cut rounds from the mix, re-flattening and re-cutting when necessary. Set aside.

Next make the soup. Make the basic stock (see page 64). Finely slice the potatoes on a mandolin. Separate the white and green parts of the leeks and finely slice each, keeping them in 2 separate piles. Take a 10cm (4-inch) square piece of muslin (cheesecloth) and place the bay leaf and clove in the middle. Tie diagonally opposite corners together to form a sealed bag.

Heat the olive oil in a saucepan and add the onion and a pinch of salt. Cook until just going soft but not coloured, then add the potatoes and cook for about 4 minutes until just softening. Add the white part of the leeks and fry gently for about 4 minutes, then add the green part of the leeks and fry for 1 minute. Add the stock and muslin (cheesecloth) bag. Bring quickly to the boil and simmer for 5–10 minutes until the potatoes are soft. Remove and discard the muslin (cheesecloth) bag. Transfer the soup to a blender and blend until smooth. Pass the soup through a sieve, adjust the seasoning if necessary (see page 15), and gently reheat while you fry the potato cakes.

Heat a little sunflower oil in a frying pan (skillet) until very hot and then add the potato cakes. Fry until golden brown and then flip over. When crispy and golden on both sides, drain on a plate lined with kitchen (paper) towel. Serve the soup hot (but not boiling) with a drizzle of oil. Add the leek and potato cakes at the end, floating in the soup like croutons.

White onions have a sweeter character and more complex flavour when cooked slowly than the more readily available brown variety. The onions bring sweetness and depth, while the olive oil provides richness and texture. I like to use a mild, buttery olive oil from Provence, as this allows the onions to sing out, but I would avoid the dominating, very peppery Spanish and Italian varieties.

This recipe calls for leek & garlic stock (see page 64). Do not be tempted to substitute this for another stock, it is a key part of the soup's character and is a very quick and easy stock to make.

Because of the slowly stewed onions the soup is quite sweet and the olive oil makes it very rich, so I have added a slightly bitter, salty garnish of roasted black olives and burnt potato to balance the dish. On their own they are too much, but they work magically with this rich, sweet soup.

Serves: 4

WHITE ONION & OLIVE OIL SOUP
with charred new potatoes, beluga lentils and black olives

FOR THE LENTILS

30g (1¼oz/3 tbsp) dried beluga lentils
300ml (10fl oz/1¼ cups) leek & garlic stock (see page 64)
3g (½ tsp) sea salt

FOR THE POTATOES

2 new potatoes
glug of extra virgin olive oil

FOR THE SOUP

4 tsp black olive crumbs (see page 115)
500ml (18fl oz/generous 2 cups) leek & garlic stock (see page 64)
500g (1lb 2oz) sliced white (or brown) onions
50ml (2fl oz/scant ¼ cup) extra virgin olive oil
25ml (1fl oz/5 tsp) top-quality extra virgin olive oil (see introduction, above)
sea salt

Soak the lentils in advance. Put the lentils in a small bowl and cover with cold water by at least 2cm (¾ inch). Place in the fridge to soak for at least 4 hours and ideally overnight. Prepare the black olive crumbs (see page 115) and leek & garlic stock (see page 64) for the lentils and soup.

Preheat the oven to (fan) 160°C/180°C/350°F/gas mark 4. Put the potatoes in a small saucepan with 400ml (13½fl oz/1⅔ cups) of water and 4g (¾ tsp) of salt. Gently bring to the boil and cover with a lid. Simmer gently for 10–20 minutes until soft, then drain.

While the potatoes are boiling, drain and rinse the lentils, then place in a small, lidded saucepan and add the stock and salt. Gently bring to the boil and cook for 15 minutes – they should be soft but hold their shape and colour. If not ready, cook for 5 minutes then check again. Once cooked, drain, discarding the stock, and keep warm.

Meanwhile, make the soup. Place the onions and 50ml (2fl oz/scant ¼ cup) of olive oil in a large saucepan. Gently heat the onions until they begin to fry and then turn down the heat. Cover with a cartouche (see page 184) and stew gently until the onions are soft. Add the stock and bring to the boil. Once boiling, remove from the heat and allow to cool slightly before adding the top-quality olive oil.

Toss the new potatoes in the olive oil, place on a small baking tray (sheet) and roast in the oven for 10 minutes. Meanwhile, transfer the soup to a blender, process until very smooth, then pass through a sieve. Return to the saucepan to gently heat through (but do not boil) and season to taste with salt (see page 15).

When the potatoes are cooked, remove from the oven and cut in half lengthways. Place on a metal tray skin side up and char until black using a blow torch. Cut each half into 6 pieces and pile neatly in the centre of each of 4 bowls. Put 1 tsp of black olive crumbs over the top and then place a few spoonfuls of lentils on top too. Pour the soup around the pile and eat straight away.

Serves: 4

CELERIAC (CELERY ROOT) SOUP

FOR THE LENTILS
15g (½oz/1½ tbsp) beluga lentils
10g (¼oz/1¼ tbsp) blanched
   hazelnuts
25ml (1fl oz/5 tsp) hazelnut oil
5ml (1 tsp) lemon juice
1g (scant ¼ tsp) sea salt
2 sprigs of thyme, leaves picked

FOR THE SALT-BAKED CELERIAC (CELERY ROOT)
1 medium celeriac (celery root)
   (at least 1kg/2¼lb)
100g (3½oz/⅓ cup) fine sea salt

FOR THE SOUP
800ml (28fl oz/3⅓ cups) basic
   stock (see page 64)
1 bay leaf
1 clove
1 piece of mace
50ml (2fl oz/scant ¼ cup) extra
   virgin olive oil
2 banana shallots, sliced
2 cloves of garlic, puréed (see
   page 147)
500g (1lb 2oz) salt-baked celeriac
   (celery root) (see above)
sea salt
tiny pinch of cayenne pepper

TO SERVE
everyday bread (see page 212)

Soak the beluga lentils a day before cooking them. Place the lentils in a bowl and cover with cold water. Leave overnight.

Make the everyday bread (see page 212) and basic stock (see page 64). Preheat the oven to (fan) 160°C/180°C/350°F/gas mark 4. Line a small baking tray (sheet) with a large sheet of foil – large enough to envelop and seal in the celeriac (celery root). Wash the celeriac (celery root) thoroughly. Pile up the salt on the foil and place the celeriac (celery root) on top. Wrap the foil up around the celeriac (celery root) to form a parcel and bake in the oven for 45 minutes to 2 hours until cooked. After 45 minutes, without unwrapping the celeriac (celery root), check if it's ready by sticking a skewer through it. If it is soft like butter it is ready. If still firm, return to the oven for 15-minute bursts until ready. When cooked, remove the foil and take the celeriac (celery root) off the salt. Set aside and leave until cool enough to handle, then cut away the skin and roots to leave the succulent flesh. Cut the flesh into 2cm (¾-inch) chunks. Weigh 500g (1lb 2oz) and reserve the rest for a garnish.

Now make the lentils. Put the hazelnuts onto a small baking tray (sheet) and roast for 5 minutes. Leave to cool, then cut into chunks roughly twice the size of a lentil. Rinse the lentils and put into a small saucepan with 1 litre (1¾ pints/4 cups) of cold water and 10g (¼oz/1¾ tsp) of salt. Bring to the boil and simmer gently with a lid on for 15 minutes until soft but still holding their shape. Drain and rinse in cold water.

Make the soup. Place the bay leaf, clove and mace in the middle of a 10cm (4-inch) square piece of muslin (cheesecloth). Tie diagonally opposite corners together to form a sealed bag. Heat the olive oil gently in a saucepan. Add the shallots and cook very gently until translucent and soft but not coloured. Add the garlic and cook for a further 3 minutes, then add the celeriac (celery root), stock and the muslin (cheesecloth) parcel and bring to a simmer. Place a lid on and gently simmer for 10 minutes to infuse. Meanwhile, in a small bowl mix the hazelnut oil, lemon and salt together then add the lentils, thyme leaves and hazelnut chunks and set aside.

Remove the soup from the heat and discard the muslin (cheesecloth) bag. Allow the soup to cool slightly and then transfer to a blender. Blend until silky smooth, then pass through a sieve. Add a tiny pinch of cayenne pepper and salt if needed (see page 15). Pour the soup into 4 soup bowls and then drizzle the lentil mix over the top, adding cooked, diced celeriac (celery root) offcuts if you wish. Serve with everyday bread.

Sunchokes are more commonly known as Jerusalem artichokes. Biologically speaking, they are not related to the more striking globe artichokes, although they do share a similar flavour profile. They are actually the root of a sunflower, and my favourite myth behind their naming is that Jerusalem is an English corruption of the Spanish girasol (sunflower), and they were named when they first came to England via Spain, after they took them from the Americas.

I prefer the name sunchoke to Jerusalem artichoke as the latter has developed something of a bad reputation over the years, largely due to the view of it as being peasant animal food. In fact, sunchokes have a wonderful, delicate flavour, refined and elegant – it is such a shame they fell out of favour.

Serves: 4

SUNCHOKE VELOUTÉ
with a mushroom duxelle garnish

FOR THE VELOUTÉ
800ml (28fl oz/3⅓ cups) basic
    stock (see page 64)
500g (1lb 2oz) sunchokes (well
    cleaned)
25ml (1fl oz/5 tsp) extra virgin olive
    oil, plus extra to drizzle
1 banana shallot, sliced
25ml (1fl oz/5 tsp) black truffle oil
sea salt

FOR THE MUSHROOM GARNISH
125g (4½oz) chestnut mushrooms
10ml (2 tsp) extra virgin olive oil
20g (¾oz) peeled and finely diced
    banana shallots
sea salt
25ml (1fl oz/5 tsp) dry white wine

TO SERVE
everyday bread (see page 212).

Make the everyday bread (see page 212) and basic stock (see page 64).

Make the velouté. Fill a bowl with 1 litre (1¾ pints/4 cups) of cold water and add the juice of half a lemon. Using a mandolin, slice the sunchokes quickly and thinly and place straight into the water. Heat the olive oil in a saucepan and add the shallot. Gently fry until just translucent and going soft. Meanwhile, drain the artichokes and pat dry. Add them to the saucepan and fry briefly, then add the stock and bring to the boil. Simmer gently with a lid on for 15–25 minutes until the artichokes are so soft they break between your fingertips. Remove from the heat and allow to cool for 10 minutes.

Next make the mushroom garnish. Chop the mushrooms into 5mm (¼-inch) dice. Heat the olive oil in a small frying pan (skillet) and add the shallots. Cook gently for about 2 minutes until just soft, but not brown. Add the diced mushrooms and a generous pinch of salt and cook until the mushrooms release their juices and these have evaporated. Add the wine and cook until the wine has completely evaporated. Remove the mushrooms from the heat and check and adjust the seasoning (see page 15). Transfer to a small bowl and keep warm while you finish the velouté.

Transfer the velouté to a blender and add the truffle oil and a little salt. Blend until silky smooth and then pass through a sieve. Check and adjust the seasoning (see page 15) and truffle oil flavour, which should not be prominent but should give a richness to the flavour.

Pour the velouté into 4 soup bowls or mugs, add a spoon of the mushroom duxelle to each bowl and a drizzle of olive oil or truffle oil and serve with the everyday bread.

This soup is rich and indulgent and shows off the flavour of the split peas at their best. You don't need to make the garnishes, although they do add another level to the soup. If you just want a nutritious bowl of soup, then simply scatter some fresh thyme and grate a little orange zest over the top when you serve it. If you do include the garnishes you will need to make the orange zest powder at least a day ahead of serving.

Serves: 4

SPLIT PEA SOUP
with salt-baked celeriac (celery root) and orange zaatar

FOR THE SOUP

50g (1¾oz) peeled shallots
50g (1¾oz) peeled carrots
50g (1¾oz) celery
50ml (2fl oz/scant ¼ cup) extra
    virgin olive oil
5g (⅛ oz) organic ginger (see
    below), finely sliced
1g (⅓ tsp) turmeric
150g (5½oz/¾ cup) yellow split
    peas
800ml (28fl oz/3⅓ cups) water
sea salt

FOR THE GARNISH

4 tsp orange zaatar (see page 119)
1 medium celeriac (celery root)
    (at least 1kg/2¼lb)
rapeseed oil, for frying
8 sprigs of thyme, leaves picked

Prepare the orange zaatar (see page 119) at least a day before making the soup.

Preheat the oven to (fan) 160°C/180°C/350°F/gas mark 4. Cook the celeriac (celery root) following the method for salt-baked celeriac (celery root) on page 57. Chop the peeled celeriac (celery root) into 1.5cm (½-inch) slices and, using a 3cm (1¼-inch) cookie cutter, cut rounds from each slice. You need 4 rounds. Cut each round in half and reserve for later.

Next make the soup. Chop the shallots, carrots and celery to 5mm (¼-inch) dice. Heat half the olive oil in a saucepan and add the diced vegetable mix and ginger. Fry gently, then turn it down to a simmer. Cover with a cartouche (see page 184) and stew very gently for up to 30 minutes, stirring occasionally, until the vegetables are melting and sweet. Remove the cartouche and discard. Add the turmeric and the split peas, stir, then add the measured water. Cover with a lid and simmer gently for 30 minutes until the split peas are completely soft.

Transfer the soup to a blender and add the rest of the olive oil. Process until silky smooth, adding a little water if needed to achieve the texture of thick double cream. Pass through a sieve, season to taste with salt (see page 15) and keep warm.

Heat a little rapeseed oil in a large frying pan (skillet) and add the celeriac (celery root) slices. Fry hard until the celeriac (celery root) is very dark and on the edge of burning on one side only.

Pour the soup into 4 soup bowls. Garnish with 2 celeriac slices and sprinkle 1 teaspoon of orange zaatar mix over the top of each bowl. Sprinkle the thyme leaves over the top, then serve straight away.

GINGER

There are two main types of ginger – the first is the most easily available from supermarkets and is very big and watery and has no real heat or character. The second is the tight, firm variety that tends to be sold as organic in health food shops. It is fiery and punchy and doesn't need peeling. If you can, track down the organic variety for this soup; if you can't then use the supermarket variety but be sure to peel it and use at least double the amount listed here.

This is a recipe I developed from the classic ribollita, the ultimate Italian peasant food. I wanted to create something even more nutritious and a little more elegant than the hearty, lumpy Tuscan bean stew. Don't get me wrong, this is still a rustic meal, but by taking your time and liberally using a really great olive oil you can make one of the most delicious things you eat this year.

Serves: 4

TUSCAN LENTIL & GRAIN BROTH

For the broth

100g (3½oz) onion

125g (4½oz) carrot

250g (9oz) celery

75ml (2¾fl oz/⅓ cup) extra virgin olive oil

8g (¼oz/1½ tsp) sea salt

4 cloves of garlic

15g (½oz/¼ cup) parsley leaves

2 x 400g (14oz) cans of whole plum tomatoes

100g (3½oz/½ cup) puy lentils

85g (3oz/½ cup) barley or spelt grain

1 litre (1¾ pints/4 cups) water

125g (4½oz) cavolo nero, cut into 5mm (¼-inch) strips

TO SERVE

8 tbsp best-quality extra virgin olive oil

black pepper

focaccia (see page 218)

Make the focaccia (see page 218).

Dice the onion, carrot and celery into 5mm (¼-inch) cubes. Put the diced vegetables into a saucepan with the olive oil and salt and gently heat. Cook very slowly, taking care not to colour the onions. Chop the garlic and parsley together to create a paste and add to the saucepan. Cook very slowly, for about 30 minutes, until the vegetables are soft.

Meanwhile, empty the cans of tomatoes into a sieve over the sink and gently rinse the sauce from them (see box, below). Shake dry, then cut into 1cm (½-inch) dice. When the vegetables are cooked, add the chopped tomatoes and any juice they released, and continue to cook gently for 20 minutes. Add the lentils, barley and water. Cook gently for about 30 minutes with a lid on, until the barley is plump and soft and the lentils are cooked. If the mix begins to run dry, add a little more water, but not too much – you want a thick broth. Add the cavolo nero and cook gently for another 15 minutes until soft, then remove from the heat. Check the seasoning and adjust if necessary (see page 15).

Spoon the broth into serving bowls and drizzle generously with the best olive oil you can find. Add a twist of black pepper and serve with focaccia.

TINNED TOMATOES

The traditional vegan recipe canon makes liberal use of canned tomatoes. They have a distinctive tomato-ish taste, but with a metallic undertone, and they pop up everywhere. For years I wouldn't go near them, associating them with a style of cookery I was desperate to break away from. Then, by chance, I stumbled on a note in a River Café cookbook that said to wash the sauce from the tomatoes before using them. It turns out the problem with canned tomatoes isn't the actual tomatoes, but the tomato sauce they are kept in. Wash this off and you have a lovely, deep tomato flavour that brings an umami depth (see page 16) without all that messy, funny-tasting sauce nonsense. Just be sure to buy good-quality whole Italian plum tomatoes, as cheap will always taste cheap.

| STOCKS |

BASIC STOCK

This basic stock is built on a foundation of those magic three ingredients: onions, celery and carrot (see box, opposite). Use this recipe as a guide, and build on the basic trio. If it is sunny, I like to use a star anise; if it is raining, I prefer the darker notes of cloves.

If you press down on the vegetables to squeeze the juices you will get the strongest flavour, but your stock will also be cloudy. This is fine if being used in a soup or risotto, but if it is for consommé then you may want to be a little more delicate.

Makes: 1 litre (1¾ pints/4 cups)

1 onion, peeled
1 carrot
1 large stick of celery
¼ slice of lemon
½ fennel bulb
1 star anise
1g (½ tsp) coriander seeds
10 black peppercorns
10g (¼oz/2½ tbsp) parsley (including stalks)
3g (1¼ tbsp) thyme (including stalks)
1 bay leaf
1.2 litres (2 pints/5 cups) water

Slice all the vegetables to a 3mm (⅛ inch) thickness. Place all the ingredients in a saucepan, cover with a lid and gently bring to the boil. Simmer for 5 minutes, then remove from the heat. Allow to cool, then strain through a fine sieve (see introduction, above).

LEEK & GARLIC STOCK

This is a great stock to emphasize the sweet depths of onion in a recipe.

Makes: 1 litre (1¾ pints/4 cups)

1 small leek, finely sliced
2 shallots, finely sliced
2 cloves of garlic, finely sliced
1 clove
1 bay leaf
1 litre (1¾ pints/4 cups) water

Put all the ingredients into a lidded saucepan and gently bring to the boil. Simmer gently for 15 minutes, then remove from the heat and leave for 15 minutes to infuse. Strain through a fine sieve.

MUSHROOM STOCK

Sometimes you need a bit of an umami kick (see page 16) to give your dish a real depth without having to add any big umami ingredients, or maybe you just want to add another layer of umami to give the dish a real punch. If that's your aim, then this is your stock, as it brings a subtle depth that doesn't overwhelm the other flavours on the plate.

As with the basic stock (see opposite), if you press down on the vegetables when straining the stock you will get a stronger flavour, but you will also have a cloudy stock.

Makes: 1 litre (1¾ pints/4 cups)

1 onion, peeled
1 carrot
1 large stick of celery
150g (5½oz) chestnut mushrooms
10 black peppercorns
10g (¼oz/2½ tbsp) parsley (including stalks)
3g (1¼ tbsp) thyme (including stalks)
2 cloves of garlic
1 bay leaf
1.2 litres (2 pints/5 cups) water
15g (½oz) dried porcini mushrooms

Slice the onion, carrot, celery and chestnut mushrooms to a 3mm (⅛ inch) thickness. Put all the ingredients, except the porcini mushrooms, into a lidded saucepan and cover with the measured water. Gently bring to the boil – it should take about 20 minutes to reach boiling point.

Once boiling, simmer very gently for 5 minutes, then remove from the heat. Immediately add the porcini mushrooms, stir to make sure they are submerged, then cover the top of the saucepan tightly with cling film (plastic wrap).

Leave the stock to cool completely, then drain off the stock through a large sieve into a clean saucepan, discarding the vegetables.

MUSHROOM & FENNEL STOCK

This is a great stock that brings a mushroom depth without an overt mushroom flavour. If you want a deeper flavour in your risotto or soup, then substitute this stock for vegetable stock.

Makes: 2 litres (3½ pints/8 cups)

2 onions, finely sliced
4 sticks of celery, finely sliced
2 fennel bulbs, finely sliced
300g (10½oz) white mushrooms, finely sliced
4 cloves of garlic, peeled
2.4 litres (4 pints/10 cups) water
2 bay leaves
4 sprigs of thyme

Put all the ingredients into a lidded saucepan and gently bring to the boil. Simmer gently for 20 minutes, then remove from the heat and leave for 30 minutes. Strain through a fine sieve.

MIREPOIX

If you are a keen cook you will probably have noticed that three vegetables keep popping up together in recipe after recipe – onion, carrot and celery. Look at most vegetable stock recipes and these three are always there. The French call it mirepoix, the Italian name is soffrito. Something about cooking these vegetables together gives the perfect depth and balance of sweetness to any dish. Simmer them in a stock for a light, fresh flavour; or fry them briefly for a sweet, vegetable flavour. Cook them long and slow in oil and something magical happens: the individual character of each vegetable breaks down and a deep, rich sweetness is achieved that is the perfect base for almost any sauce or soup. The trick is to cook them long and slow, making sure they don't dry out. You want them to break down completely – lose your nerve or allow them to colour and something will be missing. You might not know what it is, but your soup will taste decidedly ordinary.

Every recipe is only as good as the ingredients you use, but some recipes are more forgiving than others. This is one of those recipes where the quality of the ingredients used makes a substantial cumulative difference. Using Iranian pistachios (the smaller, dark green variety) will make the pâté richer and a more dramatic shade of green. Finding a buttery olive oil for the pâté will make it rich and satisfying, while using a light, grassy olive oil for the salad, such as one from Sicily, will make it light and fresh. It will, of course, be delicious should you use normal pistachios and a decent olive oil for everything, and more than worth the effort, but it will never reach the subtle, higher levels of perfection that distinguish the great from the good.

Serves: 4

PISTACHIO PÂTÉ
with orange and marjoram salad and carta di musica

FOR THE PÂTÉ

90g (3oz/²⁄₃ cup) Iranian pistachios
90ml (3¼fl oz/generous ⅓ cup) top-quality olive oil
15g (½oz/¼ cup) parsley leaves
2g (1 tsp) orange zest
1 clove of garlic
110ml (3¾fl oz/scant ½ cup) cold water
3g (scant 1 tsp) agar powder
sea salt
cayenne pepper

FOR THE ORANGE AND MARJORAM SALAD

3 oranges (a sweet seedless variety like navel is perfect)
25ml (1fl oz/5 tsp) light, grassy olive oil (see introduction)
2g (2 tsp) marjoram leaves, shredded
black pepper

FOR THE GARNISH

orange zest powder (see page 119)
carta di musica (see page 214)
4 tsp broken pistachios
few small salad leaves
few marjoram leaves

Make the orange zest powder (see page 119) and the carta di musica (see page 214).

Place a 12cm (4¾-inch) square pastry frame on a small board or plate lined with cling film (plastic wrap) or prepare 4 small pots or cups.

Put the pistachios for the pâté into a blender and process until they resemble fine breadcrumbs. Add the olive oil, parsley, orange zest and garlic and blend until combined. From here on, you need to work fast as the pâté will set quickly as it cools. Put the measured water into a small saucepan and, adding a little at a time, whisk in the agar and bring to the boil, whisking continuously to prevent the agar from catching. As soon as it boils, remove from the heat. Quickly measure the hot agar mix into the blender jug and make it back up to 110ml (3¾fl oz/scant ½ cup) by adding a little cold water if necessary. Blend until silky smooth. Taste for seasoning (see page 15) and add salt and cayenne pepper as necessary, remembering this will be served cold.

Pour the pâté into your prepared mould(s) and then cover the top with cling film (plastic wrap) in contact with the surface of the pâté to prevent a skin from forming. Place in the fridge for at least 2 hours to set firmly.

About 45 minutes before serving, make the salad. Using a sharp knife, remove the orange peel and all the white pith. Cut cleanly down the lines/membranes to remove each segment. Cut the segments into 1cm (½-inch) chunks and put into a bowl with the olive oil, marjoram and a twist of black pepper. Leave for 10–30 minutes for the flavours to come together.

Carefully remove the pâté from the mould (or serve in the pot) and cut into 4 slices. Place a slice on each of 4 starter-sized plates and add a few broken pistachios. Spoon the orange salad in a pile next to the pâté, dust the plate with pinches of orange zest powder and add a few salad and marjoram leaves and the carta di musica.

I have been making this recipe for years. It's known so many iterations it barely resembles its humble origins, but the core is always the same: en papillote carrots, with some simple aromatics, given depth and body by cashew nuts. This version leans a little to the east, but it works well with thyme, rosemary or pine, or even just bay and lemon in place of the ginger and coriander.

If you want to make this recipe without the agar then simply omit it, and the water, from the recipe; however, it won't cut into clean slices without it.

Serves: 4

CARROT & CASHEW PÂTÉ
with rye crisp breads and pickles

20g (¾oz) organic ginger (see page 60), sliced
3g (1½ tsp) coriander seeds
5 star anise
600g (1lb 5oz) peeled and trimmed large carrots
25ml (1fl oz/5 tsp) rapeseed oil
4g (¾ tsp) sea salt
100ml (3½fl oz/scant ½ cup) water (optional)
2g (generous ½ tsp) agar powder (optional)
135g (4¾oz/1 cup) cashew nuts

TO SERVE
rye crisp breads (see page 210)
tamari seeds (see page 22)
pickled carrot (see page 100)
pickled kohlrabi (see page 100)
salad leaves
edible flowers

Make the rye crisp breads (see page 210), tamari seeds (see page 22), pickled carrot (see page 100) and pickled kohlrabi (see page 100).

Preheat the oven to (fan) 160°C/180°C/350°F/gas mark 4. Oil and line a 27 x 5cm (10½ x 2 inch) terrine mould with baking parchment, leaving paper overhanging the edges so you can lift the pâté out. If you are omitting the agar, use 4 pots or tea cups.

Put the ginger, coriander seeds and star anise in a large bowl. Cut the carrots into equal-sized chunks, roughly half the size of the smallest carrot, but don't cut them too small. Add the carrots and oil to the bowl with the ginger. Sprinkle over the salt and mix well. Lay a 45cm (18-inch) length of baking parchment on a chopping board and put the carrot mix in the centre. Fold the paper in half, capturing the carrots in the middle, and roll up the edges to form a sealed half-moon shaped parcel. Place the parcel on a baking tray (sheet) and roast in the oven for 45 minutes until the carrots feel soft. When cooked, remove from the oven and leave to cool slightly.

If using agar, put the water into a small saucepan and whisk gently while slowly sprinkling in the agar. Bring up to a simmer, whisking all the time. When it reaches a gentle boil, remove from the heat and set aside.

Open the bag of carrots and take out the chunks of carrot. Remove and discard all the seeds and ginger, then put the carrots into a blender with the cashews and agar mix (if using). Blend together until very smooth with a silky texture, then pass through a sieve. Taste for salt (see page 15) and adjust as necessary, bearing in mind the mix will be served cold. While hot, spoon or pipe the mix into the prepared terrine mould, banging the mould to knock out any air. Smooth the top with a palette knife and cover with cling film (plastic wrap), in contact with the mix to prevent a skin forming. Place in the fridge for 1–2 hours to set. If made without agar, spoon or pipe it evenly between your pots, place cling film (plastic wrap) over the top in contact with the mix to prevent a skin forming, then place in the fridge for 4 hours to set.

When ready to serve, remove the cling film (plastic wrap) and turn the mould over onto a board. Remove the baking parchment and cut into 1.5cm (½-inch) slices. Serve the pâté with rye crisp breads, pickled kohlrabi, pickled carrot, tamari seeds and a few salad leaves and edible flowers, or spread on a piece of fresh bread with a light green salad for lunch.

This is a simple variation on the carrot & cashew pâté (see page 69), but with bigger, bolder flavours and a nod to northern Europe with the flavour combinations. Beetroot (beets) and carrots are very similar in terms of their structure and their starch and sugar content. The layers you can see in a beetroot (beet) are the same thing as the core and outer of a carrot, just many times over. This means that any technique that works for a carrot will almost certainly work just as well for a beetroot (beet). This pâté is delicious served with rye bread, sauerkraut and mustard.

Serves: 4–6

BEETROOT (BEETS), WALNUT & DILL PÂTÉ
with mustard and sauerkraut

100g (3½oz/1 cup) walnuts
650g (1lb 7oz) red beetroot (beets)
30ml (4fl oz/2 tbsp) water
5g (⅛ oz/1¾ tbsp) dill leaves
20ml (4 tsp) walnut oil
sea salt

TO SERVE
mustard (see page 41)
sauerkraut (see page 101)
sprigs of dill
salad leaves

Make the mustard (see page 41) 3 weeks before eating so it has time to mature, and the sauerkraut (see page 101) at least 5 days before eating.

Put the walnuts in a bowl and cover with cold water by at least 2cm (¾ inch). Leave for 6 hours or ideally overnight to soak.

Preheat the oven to (fan) 160°C/180°C/350°F/gas mark 4. Lay a 45cm (18-inch) length of foil over a deep baking tray (sheet) and put the beetroot (beets) in the centre. Bring the foil up around the beetroot (beets), add the measured water, and roll up the edges to form a sealed parcel. Roast for 45–60 minutes until soft, then remove from the oven and leave until cold. Remove and discard the beetroot (beets) skins. Cut the flesh into chunks and put into a blender. Drain the walnuts, rinse under cold water and add to the blender, along with the dill, walnut oil and a good pinch of salt.

Blend everything together until silky smooth, then ideally pass it through a sieve. Check and adjust the seasoning (see page 15). While the mix is hot, spoon or pipe it into 4–6 pots, covering the surface with cling film (plastic wrap) in contact with the pâté, to prevent a skin forming. Place in the fridge for 1–2 hours to become firm.

When ready, garnish with a sprig of dill and serve with salad leaves, sauerkraut and mustard. This is also delicious spread on rye bread.

The depth of flavour in this parfait is incredible – it's one of those dishes that people can't believe is made purely from plants. The parfait alone is well worth making, set in little pots and served with some crusty bread or carta di musica (see page 214) and a green salad. But if you want something a little more impressive, then adding the port glaze and pea salad really elevates the parfait.

Serves: 4

RICH MUSHROOM PARFAIT
with port glaze and a pea and shallot salad

FOR THE PARFAIT
30g (1¼oz) dried porcini mushrooms
300ml (10fl oz/1¼ cups) boiling water
40ml (1½fl oz/8 tsp) extra virgin olive oil
50g (1¾oz) finely sliced shallots
200g (7oz) finely sliced mushrooms
0.5g (⅔ tsp) thyme leaves
125ml (4fl oz/½ cup) port
1.5g (½ tsp) iota carrageenan powder and 1g (scant ¼ tsp) agar powder (or 2.5g (¾ tsp) agar powder)
100g (3½oz/¾ cup) pine nuts
2g (⅓ tsp) sea salt
10ml (2 tsp) truffle oil

FOR THE GLAZE
80ml (3fl oz/⅓ cup) port
40ml (1½fl oz/8 tsp) red wine vinegar
reserved mushroom stock and dried mushrooms from the parfait (see above)
1g (⅓ tsp) iota carrageenan powder (or agar powder)

FOR THE PEA SALAD
50g (1¾oz/⅓ cup) shelled fresh peas
12 sugar snap peas, ends and strings removed
32 rings of pickled shallots (see page 98)
15ml (1 tbsp) extra virgin olive oil
4 little gem lettuce leaves

Put the dried porcini mushrooms and boiling water in a jug to make a stock. Cover with cling film (plastic wrap) and leave for 45 minutes until cold. Sieve the stock, reserving the mushroom stock and two-thirds of the rehydrated mushrooms. Discard the rest of the rehydrated mushrooms.

Seal the base of a 12cm (4¾-inch) square pastry frame (or similar) with cling film (plastic wrap) and place on a small baking tray (sheet). Alternatively, use small moulds or pots.

Put the olive oil into a saucepan and heat gently. Add the shallots and fry until just soft. Add the sliced mushrooms and thyme and cook until the juices from the mushrooms have been released and evaporated. Add the port and cook to reduce to a thick syrup. Add the iota and/or agar to the mix and stir to combine, then add 160ml (5½fl oz/⅔ cup) of the reserved mushroom stock and the rehydrated mushrooms and bring to the boil. Once boiling, remove from the heat and add the pine nuts and salt. Transfer to a blender and blend until very smooth. Add the truffle oil and blend to combine, then adjust the seasoning (see page 15), remembering it will be served cold. Pour into the mould and place in the fridge for at least 2 hours to set.

When the parfait is set, make the port glaze. Put the port and red wine vinegar into a saucepan and heat to reduce by half. Measure the remaining reserved mushroom stock and make it up to 125ml (4fl oz/½ cup). Add it to the saucepan, whisk in the iota and bring to a simmer. Sieve the glaze into a jug and immediately pour over the parfait to an even 2mm (1¹⁄₁₆ inch) thickness.

Prepare the pea salad. Blanch the podded peas for 1–2 minutes, then shock in ice-cold water (see page 185). Blanch the sugar snap peas for no longer than 30 seconds, then shock in ice-cold water (see page 185). Drain all the peas and put into a small mixing bowl, then add the pickled shallots and olive oil and mix to dress.

Remove the parfait from the mould and cling film (plastic wrap). Trim the edges then cut into 4 squares with a hot knife. Place 1 piece of parfait on each of 4 plates. Place 1 lettuce leaf next to each parfait and evenly split the pea salad between them, spooning the mix into the lettuce leaf and over the plate. Serve straight away.

I have a quiet love of Germanic flavours: they are so wholesome, robust and honest. They don't have the modern style of the new Nordic foods or the sophistication of the French haute cuisine, but they bring their own comfort and taste. I particularly like to eat them when the leaves begin to fall from the trees.

Remember to allow time for the lentils to soak and the pâté to set. This is also delicious with my fennel and hazelnut salad (see page 104).

Serves: 4–6

GREEN LENTIL & ONION PÂTÉ
with rye bread, sauerkraut and mustard

FOR THE PÂTÉ

160g (5¾oz/¾ cup) dried green lentils
100ml (3½fl oz/scant ½ cup) rapeseed oil
215g (7½oz) peeled and sliced brown onions
4g (¾ tsp) sea salt
30g (1¼oz/½ cup) parsley leaves
30g (1¼oz/1 cup) spinach
4g (1¼ tsp) agar powder (optional)
80ml (3fl oz/⅓ cup) water

TO SERVE

rye bread (see page 209)
sauerkraut (see page 101)
mustard (see page 41)

Make the mustard (see page 41) 3 weeks before you need it so it can mature, and the sauerkraut (see page 101) 5 days before serving.

Put the dried green lentils into a bowl and cover with cold water by at least 2.5cm (1 inch). Put into the fridge and leave to soak for at least 4 hours or overnight.

Make the rye bread (see page 209).

Drain the lentils and rinse under cold water. Put into a small saucepan, cover with cold water (do not add salt), and bring to the boil. Simmer gently until soft but not broken down – you want a pleasing "pop" in the mouth with no grainy texture. Drain and shock with ice-cold water (see page 185) before draining again. Measure out 215g (7½oz) and 80g (3oz) of the cooked lentils and set aside until needed.

Heat the rapeseed oil in a small saucepan and add the onions and salt. Turn down the heat to low and cook gently, stirring often, until they are jelly-like in texture but not coloured. Add the parsley and spinach and turn over to wilt briefly. Add the agar, if using, and stir in thoroughly. Add the water and 215g (7½oz) of the cooked green lentils and heat for about 3 minutes until the lentils are too hot to touch.

Put the lentil and spinach mixture into a blender and process until the mixture is smooth but with flecks of parsley still visible. Working quickly before the agar sets, add the remaining 80g (3oz) of cooked lentils to the mix and stir to combine. Spoon into 4–6 glass containers and cover with cling film (plastic wrap) to prevent a skin from forming. Put into the fridge for 4 hours to set.

Serve the pâté, spread on rye bread, with sauerkraut and mustard.

This is a very simple, clean recipe that tastes of a light ethereal squash. I have used butternut as it is widely available and very consistent, but you can experiment with other varieties of squash. Crown prince is especially good, but beware of some of the watery pumpkins as you'll need to cook the water out of them for a long time so the mousse isn't too wet at the end.

Serves: 4

BUTTERNUT MOUSSE

500g (1lb 2oz) peeled butternut squash, chopped into 2cm (¾-inch) chunks
2 cloves of garlic, peeled but whole
1 banana shallot, sliced
25ml (1fl oz/5 tsp) extra virgin olive oil
4 sprigs of rosemary
4g (¾ tsp) sea salt
1g (⅓ tsp) xanthan gum
100ml (3½fl oz/scant ½ cup) aquafaba (see box, below)

TO SERVE
kimchi (see page 101)
flat breads (see page 217)
tamari seeds (see page 22), optional

Make the kimchi (see page 101) at leat 5 days in advance.

Make the flat breads (see page 217) and the tamari seeds (see page 22), if using.

Preheat the oven to (fan) 160°C/180°C/350°F/gas mark 4. Mix together all the ingredients except the xanthan and aquafaba and spread out on a large baking tray (sheet). Cover with foil and roast for 25–35 minutes until the squash is soft. Pick out the garlic and rosemary and discard.

Put the rest of the mix into a blender with the xanthan and blend until very smooth. Transfer to a large frying pan (skillet) and cook over a medium heat until very thick (like whipped cream). Transfer to a large bowl and cover with cling film (plastic wrap) in contact with the surface of the mix to prevent a skin forming. Place in the fridge for at least 2 hours or overnight.

When the purée is chilled, put the aquafaba into a clean mixing bowl and whisk with an electric whisk to stiff peaks. Remove the purée from the fridge and stir a third of the aquafaba into the purée with a silicon spatula, then gently fold in another third. Finally fold in the rest of the aquafaba. Place in 4 pots or tea cups and refrigerate until needed.

Serve with kimchi, flat breads and some tamari seeds if you like.

AQUAFABA

I refused to even try aquafaba for a long time, treating it as I do all substitutes, with barely concealed contempt. Aquafaba is the water left after you have cooked legumes. The proteins from the legumes transfer to the cooking water and behave exactly like the proteins in egg whites, forming stable foams and meringues and can be used in exactly the same quantities. When first experimenting simply open a can of chickpeas (garbanzo beans) and use the water from this, ensuring it is not salted. As you get more confident you can make your own. Simply soak 400g (14oz) of beans or chickpeas (garbanzo beans) overnight in cold water and refresh. Put in a lidded saucepan with 1.8 litres (3¼ pints/7½ cups) of water and simmer for about 60 minutes until cooked. Allow to cool in the water, then strain out the beans and the remaining water is aquafaba. You can reduce it further to make it even stronger, but its beany flavour will be more pronounced.

There are two ways of treating asparagus: as a fresh, green vegetable like peas; or for a darker flavour experience, like a cabbage. If you want it fresh, simply blanch and enjoy with something tart such as lemon aioli. If you treat it like a cabbage, then you're best off charring it (see the Maillard reaction, page 177). This recipe makes liberal use of the cabbage connection, and coupled with onions and dark spring greens it's as far from the fresh green version as you can get – it's also seductively delicious.

Serves: 4

CHARRED ASPARAGUS
with a cannelini bean and onion purée

FOR THE BEAN PURÉE
100g (3½oz) finely sliced brown onions
25ml (1fl oz/5 tsp) extra virgin olive oil
100g (3½oz/½ cup) cooked cannellini beans (good-quality canned beans are fine)
25ml (1fl oz/5 tsp) best-quality (preferably Italian) extra virgin olive oil
20ml (4 tsp) lemon juice
sea salt

FOR THE ASPARAGUS PARCELS
20 asparagus spears
4 large spring green leaves
rapeseed oil, to fry

FOR THE GARNISH
20 pickled shallot rounds (see page 98)
cabbage powder (see page 118)

Make the pickled shallots (see page 98) and cabbage powder (see page 118) in advance. The purée is also best made the day before you need it.

To make the purée, heat the onions and regular extra virgin olive oil in a small saucepan. Stew gently for about 25 minutes until the onions are meltingly soft but not coloured, then transfer to a blender and add the cannellini beans, best-quality olive oil and lemon juice. Season well with salt and blend for 3–4 minutes until silky smooth. Check and adjust the seasoning (see page 15). Transfer to an airtight container and store in the fridge for at least 4 hours to firm up. (The purée will keep in the fridge for up to 3 days.) When ready to cook, transfer the purée into a piping bag and leave to come to room temperature.

Blanch the asparagus for 2 minutes and shock in ice-cold water (see page 185). Blanch the spring green leaves for 30 seconds and shock in ice-cold water (see page 185). Cut 4 x 1cm (½-inch) wide strips from the spring green leaves, each long enough to wrap around 5 asparagus spears. Separate the asparagus into 4 piles of 5 spears and wrap each pile together using 1 spring green strip for each parcel – the strip should just stick to itself.

Heat a splash of rapeseed oil in a large frying pan (skillet) until smoking hot. Add the asparagus parcels and fry hard on one side until very dark in colour and burnt in places. Carefully turn over and colour on each side until they are evenly coloured all round.

Place 1 asparagus parcel onto each of 4 starter-size plates. Pipe about 3 tablespoons of the cannellini bean purée into a neat pile next to the asparagus and arrange 5 of the pickled shallot rings on each plate.

Put the cabbage powder into the centre of a 20cm (8-inch) square piece of muslin (cheesecloth), bring the corners together to form a parcel and tie it to form a shaker, or use a small, fine sieve. Sprinkle the cabbage powder over the bean purée and around the plate, then serve straight away.

Traditionally, this recipe uses calçots, a long, Catalonian variety of onion that is very hard to source anywhere else in the world. However, this recipe is delicious with young leeks substituted in their place. In an ideal world you would cook the charred leeks on a barbecue. The outer leaves of the leeks burn and protect the inner layers that cook slowly and become melting and sweet. You can create a similar effect with a griddle pan – just make sure you have the kitchen extractor fan on full!

This dish is really about sharing and indulging, refining the recipe will only damage its character, so find a bottle of rustic red table wine, bake a loaf of crusty bread and enjoy in the sunshine.

Serves: 4

CHARRED BABY LEEKS
with romesco sauce

For the charred leeks
8–12 baby leeks

FOR THE ROMESCO SAUCE
1 bulb of garlic
100ml (3½fl oz/scant ½ cup) extra virgin olive oil, plus extra to drizzle
2 red (bell) peppers
25g (1oz/3 tbsp) blanched hazelnuts
25g (1oz/2¾ tbsp) almonds
30ml (1fl oz/2 tbsp) sherry vinegar
5g (⅛oz/2 tsp) smoked paprika
1g (generous ½ tsp) cayenne pepper
5g (1 tsp) sea salt

Preheat the oven to (fan) 160°C/180°C/350°F/gas mark 4. Wash the leeks and trim the dark green tops, leaving the roots intact.

Cut the base from the garlic bulb to expose the cloves. Drizzle with a little olive oil and put onto a small baking tray (sheet). Roast in the oven for 15 minutes or until soft and lightly coloured, then remove from the oven and leave to cool. Squeeze the bottom of the bulb to pop the cloves out and put the cloves into a blender.

Rub the red peppers with the measured olive oil and place on a baking tray (sheet). Roast in the oven for 30–40 minutes until the skin blackens and blisters but the peppers aren't mushy. Remove from the oven and put in a small bowl. Cover with cling film (plastic wrap), leave until cold, then peel off the skin and remove the stem and any seeds. Roughly chop the flesh and add to the blender.

Mix the hazelnuts and almonds together and put on a small baking tray (sheet). Roast in the oven for 5–7 minutes until golden but not very dark. Transfer to the blender. Add the rest of the ingredients to the blender and blend until very smooth. Check and adjust the seasoning (see page 15).

Heat a large griddle pan until very hot. Add the leeks and leave until the underside begins to blacken. Turn them over by a quarter and repeat. Keep turning them over by a quarter until the whole leek is blackened and the inside is melting, then remove from the griddle and allow to cool slightly. Cut off the outer charred layer and peel away, leaving just the succulent soft middle.

Serve the leeks with the romesco sauce. Delicious with a crusty loaf of bread and a robust red wine.

Courgettes (zucchini) are one of my favourite vegetables, both to eat and grow. Nurture one plant and you'll have more than you can eat all through the season. This dish makes use of courgettes (zucchini) when they are, in my opinion, best to eat – small and sweet, no bigger than your forefinger. If they are bigger than this, then you'll have to trim them down to smaller pieces, perhaps into batons. Either way, this is a fresh, delicious plate of summer.

Serves: 4

FINGERLING COURGETTES (ZUCCHINI)
with lemon and mint ice and garden herb purée

FOR THE LEMON AND MINT ICE
100g (3½oz/½ cup) caster (superfine) sugar
250ml (8½fl oz/1 cup) water
35g (1¼oz/1½ cups) mint leaves
80ml (3fl oz/⅓ cup) lemon juice

FOR THE HERB PURÉE
175ml (6fl oz/¾ cup) extra virgin olive oil
150g (5½oz) banana shallots, sliced
100g (3½oz/3⅓ cups) spinach, coarsely chopped
50g (1¾oz/1 cup) chives, coarsely chopped
100g (3½oz/1⅔ cups) parsley leaves, coarsely chopped
50ml (2fl oz/scant ¼ cup) cold water
10ml (2 tsp) black truffle oil
sea salt

FOR THE CHARRED COURGETTES (ZUCCHINI)
12 finger-sized courgettes (zucchini), with flowers if possible
60ml (2¼fl oz/¼ cup) extra virgin olive oil
2 cloves of garlic, peeled and cut in half lengthways

First make the lemon and mint ice as it needs 4 hours to freeze. Put the sugar and water into a small saucepan and bring to the boil, then remove from the heat and add the mint. Leave to infuse until it cools to room temperature, then add the lemon juice. Pass through a sieve into a small container and freeze for 4 hours (or until frozen solid). Use a fork to scrape the ice into a fine powder/mushy texture. Return to the freezer.

To make the purée, heat 25ml (1fl oz/5 tsp) of the olive oil in a large saucepan. Add the shallots and cook until soft and translucent. Add the spinach, chives and parsley and stir until the spinach has wilted, then tip onto a large baking tray (sheet), spread out and leave to cool. Once cool, transfer to a blender. Add the water and the rest of the olive oil and blend until smooth and glossy (don't add extra water). Once completely smooth, add the truffle oil and blend to mix. Pass through a sieve into a bowl and season to taste (see page 15). Cover with cling film (plastic wrap) in contact with the surface to prevent a skin forming and place in the fridge to chill.

Remove the courgette (zucchini) flowers, pinch out the stamen and discard, and set aside. Blanch the courgettes (zucchini) for 3–5 minutes, until just softening, then shock in ice-cold water (see page 185). Pat dry, then cut each courgette (zucchini) in half lengthways. Heat the olive oil in a saucepan and add the garlic. Cook gently for 2 minutes, then turn down the heat. Add the halved courgettes (zucchini) and heat very gently without frying until warm.

Pour a little of the herb purée in a round blob on each plate and add 6 courgette (zucchini) pieces and add 1 tablespoon of lemon mint ice. Tear the reserved courgette (zucchini) flowers into strips and scatter across each plate. Serve straight away.

Red peppers can be a tricky ingredient to use. They are delicious, sweet and succulent, but they can also lack a level of sophistication, and their sweetness is almost too much when they are central to a dish. Here I have used the earthy flavour of broad beans (fava beans) and garlic to balance them.

Serves: 4

ROASTED RED PEPPERS
with broad beans (fava beans) and stewed tomatoes

FOR THE BROAD BEANS (FAVA BEANS)

100g (3½oz/⅔ cup) whole dried broad beans (fava beans)

400g (14oz) plum tomatoes

4g (¾ tsp) sea salt

60ml (2¼fl oz/¼ cup) extra virgin olive oil

50g (1¾oz) spring onions (scallions), finely sliced

10g (¼oz/2⅔ tbsp) parsley leaves, finely chopped

2g (scant 1 tsp) smoked paprika

10ml (2 tsp) red wine vinegar

100g (3½oz/3⅓ cups) baby spinach leaves

FOR THE PEPPERS

1 x quantity of broad bean (fava bean) purée (see page 184)

4 Romano red peppers

2g (1 tsp) fennel seeds

extra virgin olive oil

sea salt

FOR THE GARNISH

2 spring onions (scallions), finely sliced

8 pitted green olives, sliced

parsley leaves

extra virgin olive oil, to drizzle

black pepper

First soak the beans. Put the whole broad beans (fava beans) into a small bowl and cover with cold water by at least 2cm (¾ inch). Leave to soak for at least 6 hours or ideally overnight. Soak the split broad beans (fava beans) for the broad bean (fava bean) purée (see page 184).

Preheat the oven to (fan) 160°C/180°C/350°F/gas mark 4. Cut the top off the Romano red peppers, then cut in half lengthways and remove and discard the seeds. Place the halved peppers in a bowl. Add the fennel seeds, a good glug of olive oil and a few pinches of salt and mix well. Place a 60cm (24-inch) strip of baking parchment on a baking tray (sheet) and place the peppers in the middle. Fold the paper in half and roll up the edges to make a sealed parcel. Bake for 30 minutes until soft, then leave to cool. Remove from the bag and discard the juice.

Drain and rinse the whole broad beans (fava beans) in cold water, then put into a small saucepan with 500ml (18fl oz/2 cups) of cold water. Bring to the boil and simmer for 45 minutes until soft but not broken up, adding more water if necessary. Once cooked, drain and rinse. Meanwhile, prepare the broad bean (fava bean) purée (see page 184).

Remove the stem of each plum tomato, then cut a cross in the skin at the bottom. Blanch the tomatoes in boiling water until the skin starts to split, then shock in ice-cold water (see page 185). Peel off the skins, cut each tomato in half and discard the seeds. Chop into 7mm (⅓ inch) dice. Put the tomatoes, salt and olive oil into a large frying pan (skillet) and simmer gently for 5 minutes. Add the spring onion (scallion) and simmer until the tomatoes have broken down, then add the parsley and broad beans (fava beans.) Simmer gently to warm. Add the smoked paprika and vinegar and stir to combine. Set aside.

Lay the pepper halves out and spread a thin layer of the broad bean (fava bean) purée down the middle, stopping 2cm (¾ inch) from the top and bottom. Roll each pepper up lengthways into a tight spiral. Cut each pepper in half widthways and place the pieces, cut side up, on a lined baking tray (sheet). Drizzle with a little olive oil and place in the oven for 10 minutes to heat.

Gently reheat the tomato and broad bean (fava bean) mixture and add the spinach, folding it over gently until the spinach is just wilted, then remove from the heat. Check and adjust the seasoning (see page 15).

Put a quarter of the bean mix on each of 4 starter-sized plates. Arrange 4 rolls of roasted pepper on each plate. Sprinkle with the spring onions (scallions), green olives and parsley leaves and add a drizzle of olive oil and a twist of black pepper. Serve straight away.

This dish is all about the subtle textures. Yes, the flavours are bold and clear, but it is the soft bite of the beetroot (beet) slivers with the creamy cashews and the crunch of the pickled beetroot (beets) that makes it stand out. It's a great dish, simple, clean and delicious. Just allow two days to make the cashew purée.

If you want to make a larger meal, then toss the beetroot (beet) slivers with some light salad leaves, thin the cashew purée to a thick cream consistency with water, and drizzle it all over, using the vierge as the salad dressing, then serve it with a slice of sourdough for a nutritious lunch.

Serves: 4

CHIOGGIA BEETROOT (BEET) SLIVERS
with aged cashew purée and lavender beetroot (beet) vierge

FOR THE CASHEW PURÉE
250g (9oz/2 cups) cashew nuts
2.5g (1 tsp) onion powder
    (see page 118)
1 acidophilus capsule
200ml (7fl oz/generous ¾ cup)
    water
5g (⅛ oz/1 tsp) sea salt

FOR THE VIERGE DRESSING
1g (½ tsp) coriander seeds
50ml (2fl oz/scant ¼ cup) lavender
    oil (see page 220)
20ml (4 tsp) lemon juice
10 tarragon leaves, diced
15–20g (½–¾oz) pickled beetroot
    (beets) (see page 98), diced

**FOR THE BEETROOT (BEET)
SLIVERS**
2 large Chioggia beetroots (beets)
    (or 4 small)
1 clove
2g (1 tsp) coriander seeds
2g (1 tsp) black peppercorns
10g (¼oz) tarragon
5g (⅛ oz) sprigs of thyme
2 bay leaves
10g (¼oz/1¾ tsp) sea salt
100ml (3½fl oz/scant ½ cup) cold
    water

FOR THE GARNISH
selection of small salad leaves

You will need to prepare the cashew purée over 2 days. Put the cashews in a small bowl, cover with cold water and leave to soak for 2 hours. Prepare the pickled beetroot (beets) (see page 98) and onion powder (see page 118).

Strain the cashews, place in a blender and add the contents of the acidophilus capsule and the water. Blend to a very smooth paste, then put into a sterilized (see page 101) lidded container. Leave somewhere warm (22°C/71°F) for 24 hours. When ready, it should smell sweet and sharp and have a foamy texture. If it isn't ready, leave for a further 12–24 hours. (If it smells rancid or has developed mould you'll have to start again.)

Make the vierge dressing at least 2 hours before serving. Crush the coriander seeds using a pestle and mortar, then put all the vierge ingredients, except the diced pickled beetroot (beets), into a small saucepan and bring to the boil. Pour this over the beetroot (beets) dice and leave for 2 hours, then strain.

When the fermented cashew is ready, place it in the blender with the salt and onion powder and blend until very smooth. Transfer to the fridge.

Preheat the oven to (fan) 160°C/180°C/350°F/gas mark 4. Take a large sheet of foil and place a similar sized sheet of baking parchment on top. Put both on a baking tray (sheet). Wash the beetroots (beets) carefully. Place the clove, coriander seeds, peppercorns, tarragon, thyme, bay leaves and salt on the centre of the baking parchment and the beetroots (beets) on top. Half form a parcel so liquid cannot escape, then pour over the measured water. Seal the parcel tightly. Place in the oven and bake for 35 minutes, then remove from the oven and open the parcel. Check the beetroot (beets) are tender – a knife should pass through them easily. If they are not ready, return to the oven in 15-minute bursts until done. Allow to cool in the parcel, then rub off the skin and discard. Set a mandolin to a 7mm (⅓ inch) setting and carefully slice the beetroots (beets) into slivers (don't worry if they break up a little bit).

Place 2 tablespoons of cashew purée on each of 4 starter-sized plates and then swipe each blob with the back of the spoon. Split the beetroot (beet) slices into 4 portions and then split each pile in 3, there should be 4–6 slices (no more) in each pile. Carefully fold each pile over like a taco and place 3 piles along the centre of the plate between the cashew purée. Arrange salad leaves in among this and then dress the whole dish with the vierge and garnish with salad leaves. Serve immediately.

The ajo blanco provides a wonderful, zingy foil for the deep flavour of the burnt spring greens. I sieve the ajo blanco to a smooth consistency so it resembles a sauce more than the traditional soup in order to make this rustic peasant dish refined and elegant. However, if you want your meal a little heartier, then sieve it a little coarser, or, for the full rustic experience, not at all.

The ajo blanco is best made a day before eating (you will therefore need to soak the almonds two days ahead) to allow the garlic and vinegar to mellow – if you serve it when you've just made it the garlic will be very strong and pronounced.

Serves: 4

BURNT SUMMER BEAN PARCEL
with confit potatoes and ajo blanco

FOR THE AJO BLANCO
200g (7oz/1½ cups) whole
    almonds
2 cloves of garlic, peeled, cut in half
    and stem removed
350ml (12fl oz/1½ cups) cold water
100ml (3½fl oz/scant ½ cup) extra
    virgin olive oil
25ml (1fl oz/5 tsp) sherry vinegar
5g (⅛oz/1 tsp) sea salt

FOR THE CONFIT POTATOES
200g (7oz) new potatoes
2g (⅓ tsp) sea salt
good-quality olive oil

FOR THE SPRING GREEN PARCELS
2 brown onions, thinly sliced
50ml (2fl oz/scant ¼ cup) extra
    virgin olive oil
2g (⅓ tsp) sea salt
6g (⅛oz/1⅓ tbsp) chopped
    summer savory (or 7g (¼oz/
    2¾ tbsp) chopped tarragon)
4 large, dark, spring green leaves
40 untrimmed green beans
rapeseed oil, to fry

FOR THE GARNISH
1 x quantity of spring green crisps
    (see page 28)

Soak the almonds 2 days in advance of cooking. Put 150g (5½oz/1 cup) of the almonds into a small bowl and cover with cold water by at least 2cm (¾ inch). Put into the fridge and leave overnight.

Preheat the oven to (fan) 160°C/180°C/350°F/gas mark 4. Place the remaining almonds on a baking tray (sheet) and roast in the oven for 8 minutes.

Drain and rinse the soaked almonds, then put all the ajo blanco ingredients into a blender and process for 1–2 minutes until completely smooth and creamy. Line a sieve with a 45cm (18-inch) square piece of muslin (cheesecloth) set over a jug. Pour the almond mix into the muslin (cheesecloth) and collect up the corners to make a bag. Squeeze to extract the ajo blanco into the jug. Keep squeezing until you are struggling to get much liquid out, then discard the bag. (The ajo blanco will keep in the fridge for up to 3 days.)

Make the spring green crisps (see page 28).

Trim the new potatoes into neat, squared-off shapes, removing the skin as you do so, then chop into 5mm (¼-inch) dice. Mix with the salt and leave for 30 minutes until a little juice is released. Drain off the liquid and put the potatoes in a small saucepan. Just cover with olive oil and simmer very gently over a low heat for about 10 minutes until the potatoes are just soft, checking them regularly. Strain the potatoes from the oil and allow the potatoes to cool to room temperature.

Make the filling for the parcels. Put the onions, olive oil and salt into a small saucepan and heat very gently until the onions are soft but not coloured. Spread out on a plate and leave to cool completely. Once cold, mix in the summer savory.

Trim the spring green leaves and then cut the central stem out, leaving 8 large half-strips of leaf. Blanch the spring green leaves for 30 seconds, then shock in ice-cold water (see page 185). Blanch the green beans for 2 minutes, then shock in ice-cold water (see page 185). Dry the beans and spring green leaves with kitchen (paper) towel. Select the best 4 spring green leaves.

continued on next page>>

<< continued from previous page

HIGH PROTEIN SAUCES

Putting vegetables at the centre of the plate creates beautiful, elegant and delicious food, but it can leave more traditional diners asking where the protein is. Leaving aside the fact that, per calorie, many plants have more protein than meats, one of my favourite tricks is to use high-calorie and high-protein foods in sauces and garnishes, inverting the traditional hierarchy of nutrients. The Mediterranean is a wonderful inspiration for this idea, with a treasure trove of traditional sauces made from nuts and seeds, from romesco and pesto to this wonderful cold soup made from almonds, garlic and olive oil.

Lay 1 leaf across a chopping board with the straight edge towards the top. Place 10 green beans in a pile on the leaf with the stalk end just sticking over the bottom, uneven edge of the leaf by about 5mm (¼ inch) and the pointed end extending at least 2cm (¾ inch) over the top. Trim the leaf if necessary.

Place a tablespoon of the onion mix on top of the pile of beans. Fold over one side of the leaf and then tightly roll the beans into a parcel, a little like sushi, to form a very tight bundle with the beans sticking out of the top and bottom. The leaf should stick to itself and hold the parcel together. Trim the parcel at the bottom to remove the bottom of the stalks and leave a clean crisp edge. Set to one side and repeat 3 more times.

Heat a little rapeseed oil in a frying pan (skillet) until very hot, almost smoking. Place the parcels in the pan with the sealed flap on the bottom, pressing them down to flatten against the pan. Fry very hard until the cabbage is almost burnt. Do not fiddle with them, you do not want to risk them falling apart. Carefully turn them over and repeat on the other side.

Place 1 parcel in the centre of each of 4 small bowls. Pile a tablespoon of confit potatoes next to the parcel, add the ajo blanco and lay a spring green crisp across the top.

This dish is an example of how to take the most humble of ingredients and raise it to the uppermost heights with careful presentation and premium treatment. Donkey carrots are the large, misshapen carrots most supermarkets reject, but they are the sweetest of the carrots and cost almost nothing.

This is a very involved dish with multiple components that require two days of preparation, but the end result is a dish that makes the humble rejected carrot taste like the finest thing you have ever eaten.

Serves: 4

ROASTED DONKEY CARROTS
with cashew cheese and seeded buckwheat

FOR THE CASHEW CHEESE

250g (9oz/2 cups) cashew nuts

3 acidophilus capsules

25ml (1fl oz/5 tsp) water

10ml (2 tsp) extra virgin olive oil

4g (¾ tsp) sea salt

10g (¼oz/scant ¼ cup) chives, finely sliced

10g (¼oz/2⅔ tbsp) parsley leaves, very finely chopped

FOR THE BUCKWHEAT

50g (1¾oz/⅓ cup) hulled buckwheat

30ml (1fl oz/2 tbsp) rapeseed oil

20g (¾oz/2½ tbsp) sunflower seeds

FOR THE ROASTED CARROTS

0.1g (pinch) saffron

40ml (1½fl oz/8 tsp) boiling water

4 large, organic donkey carrots, washed thoroughly

2 star anise

1g (½ tsp) coriander seeds

25ml (1fl oz/5 tsp) extra virgin olive oil

3g (½ tsp) sea salt, plus extra to sprinkle

rapeseed oil, to fry

truffle oil, to drizzle

FOR THE GARNISH

20 strips of pickled carrot (see page 100)

black truffle, grated (optional)

First prepare the cashew cheese as it takes 2 days to make. Put the cashews in a small bowl and cover with cold water. Leave for 2 hours (no longer), then drain and place in a blender with the contents of the acidophilus capsules. Add the measured water and olive oil and blend. If too dry, add just a little more water – you need a firm mix you can shape. Line a sieve with a muslin (cheesecloth) and set it over a bowl. Add the cashew mix, then fold the muslin (cheesecloth) over and cover it with cling film (plastic wrap). Leave somewhere warm (22°C/71°F) for 24 hours, until it smells sweetly sour and 'cheesy'. Transfer the cashew cheese mix to a blender and process until smooth, then place in an airtight container in the fridge for 4 hours to firm up. Prepare the pickled carrot (see page 100).

When the cheese has chilled, add the salt and mix well, then transfer to a piping bag with a 1.5cm (½-inch) round nozzle (tip). Put the chives and parsley onto a plate and mix together. Pipe a 10cm (4-inch) long sausage of the cashew mix onto the herbs and gently roll it, taking care not to damage its shape.

Lay out a 15cm (6-inch) long strip of cling film (plastic wrap) and, using a palette knife, transfer the cashew sausage onto it. Carefully fold the cling film (plastic wrap) over and roll the sausage tightly in it. Twist one end and then the other to tighten the shape, taking care not to trap any air inside. Put the sausage into the fridge and repeat with the mix, piping and rolling until you have 4 sausages. Leave these in the fridge for 24 hours to become really firm. (Any leftover mix makes a great spread on toast.)

Put the buckwheat into a bowl and cover with cold water. Leave to soak for 2 hours, then drain and rinse. Fill a saucepan with 2 litres (3½ pints/8 cups) of water and 20g (¾oz/1¼ tbsp) of salt and bring to the boil. Add the buckwheat and cook for 3–5 minutes until just softening (be careful not to overcook it). Drain and rinse in cold water, then set aside.

Put the saffron into a small bowl and pour the boiling water over it. Leave for 30 minutes. Preheat the oven to (fan) 160°C/180°C/350°F/gas mark 4.

Cut 6 diagonal scores 5mm (¼ inch) deep along one side of a carrot. Turn over and repeat on the other side. Repeat with the rest of the carrots. Take a 45cm (18-inch) length of baking parchment and lay it across a deep baking tray (sheet). Lay the carrots across the middle of the paper and add the rest of the roasted carrots ingredients except the rapeseed oil and truffle oil. Mix together and then fold the bag over and roll up the edges to form a sealed parcel. Bake in the oven for 45 minutes to 1 hour until the carrots are meltingly soft but not coloured.

Allow the carrots to cool completely in the bag, then remove them from the aromatic mix. Cut each carrot in half lengthways. Turn down the oven to (fan) 140°C/160°C/310°F/gas mark 2½.

Take each half of carrot and lay it flat, face up, in front of you. Using a sharp knife, cut scores diagonally all along it approximately 4mm (¼ inch) apart and 4mm (¼ inch) deep. Then cut scores diagonally in the other direction to form a cross hatch. Repeat this for all the halves.

Heat a little rapeseed oil in a large frying pan (skillet) until very hot. Add the carrot halves, in batches if necessary, and press down firmly so the whole face is in contact with the pan. When almost blackened, place on a small baking tray (sheet), face down, and put in the oven for 5 minutes to warm through fully. After 5 minutes, remove from the oven and turn the carrots face up. Sprinkle a little salt over each one and then drizzle generously with truffle oil, flexing each carrot slightly to open up the cross hatch.

Heat the rapeseed oil for the buckwheat in a small frying pan (skillet). Add the sunflower seeds and fry gently until a dark golden colour but not burnt. Add the cooked buckwheat and stir to mix and warm through.

Place 1 piece of carrot on each of 4 plates. Remove the cling film (plastic wrap) from each cashew "sausage" (rolling it gently to re-form the shape if necessary) and place the "sausage" next to the carrot along with a couple of tablespoons of buckwheat. Add 5 rolls of pickled carrot, and, if using, grate black truffle generously across the carrot. Serve immediately.

This recipe plays on the idea that Jerusalem artichokes and sunflower seeds are both from the sunflower family. The artichokes are the root and the seeds are, well, the seed. As is so often the case with members of the same family, the flavours go wonderfully together, balanced by the bitter acidity of the grapefruit. This recipe comes courtesy of Steven Yates.

Serves: 4–6

ROAST JERUSALEM ARTICHOKES
with sunflower seed purée and pink grapefruit gel

FOR THE ARTICHOKES
8 Jerusalem artichokes
2 bay leaves
5g (¹⁄₈ oz/2 tbsp) thyme leaves
5g (¹⁄₈ oz/1 tsp) sea salt, plus extra
    to sprinkle
20ml (4 tsp) rapeseed oil
sunflower oil, for frying and
    deep-fat frying

FOR THE GRAPEFRUIT GEL
4g (generous 1 tsp) agar powder
40g (1½oz/3⅓ tbsp) caster
    (superfine) sugar
190ml (6½fl oz/generous ¾ cup)
    pink grapefruit juice
25ml (1fl oz/5 tsp) white wine

FOR THE PURÉE
1 x quantity of sunflower seed
    purée (see page 185)

FOR THE GRAPEFRUIT SEGMENTS
1–2 pink grapefruit

FOR THE GARNISH
micro red sorrel

Preheat the oven to (fan) 160°C/180°C/350°F/gas mark 4. Clean the artichokes thoroughly with a brush. Lay out a 45cm (18-inch) length of baking parchment and put the artichokes into the centre. Scatter the rest of the artichoke ingredients (except the sunflower oil) over the artichokes. Fold the paper in half capturing the ingredients in the middle and roll up the edges, to form a sealed half-moon shaped parcel.

Place the parcel on a small baking tray (sheet) and roast for 20–30 minutes until the artichokes feel soft when pushed through the outside of the bag, but aren't coloured. Allow the bag to cool for 5 minutes and then carefully open and remove the artichokes. Cut each artichoke in half lengthways, pat dry and sprinkle with a pinch of salt. Reserve 2 roasted artichokes to make artichoke crisps.

Make the sunflower seed purée (see page 185). Make the grapefruit gel. Mix the agar with the sugar. Put the grapefruit juice and white wine into a small saucepan and whisk the sugar and agar mix in slowly. Put the saucepan onto the heat and gently bring to a simmer, whisking to stop the agar from sticking. As soon as it starts to simmer, remove from the heat and pour into a small container. Cover and put into the fridge for 30 minutes. Once set firmly, transfer to a small blender and blend until completely smooth. Transfer to a piping bag.

Prepare the grapefruit segments. Using a sharp knife, peel off the grapefruit skin and white pith. Cut cleanly down each side of the membranes, working round the fruit to remove each segment (you need 3 per person), then place on kitchen (paper) towel. Spread the grapefruit segments out on a metal tray and, using a blowtorch, burn the upward face (you can skip this step but it is a nice touch).

Prepare your deep-fat fryer (see page 26). Cut the 2 reserved roasted artichokes in half lengthways and scoop as much flesh out as you can. Fry the skins until golden brown, then drain on kitchen (paper) towel and sprinkle with a little salt.

Heat a little rapeseed oil in a frying pan (skillet) until very hot. Put the artichokes face down in the pan and cook until very well done but not quite burnt.

Put 2 tablespoons of sunflower seed purée on each of 4 starter-size plates and spread it out slightly, then spread the purée across the plate in one confident motion. Add the roasted artichokes and grapefruit segments on top of the purée. Dot pink grapefruit gel around the plate and add red sorrel leaves and an artichoke crisp. Serve straight away.

| PICKLES |

Traditionally pickling was used as a way of preserving crops for the winter, but in today's world of easily available ingredients year round there is little need unless you have your own garden. This tradition has left us with a wonderful culinary tool; pickles add acidity, sweetness and texture to a plate, helping to balance dishes, particularly when they are very fatty or rich.

Traditional pickles are designed to preserve food without refrigeration and so are very high in acidity, and/or sugar, and this can present a problem when balancing delicate plates of food, or pairing them with wine. I tend to water down the pickling liquid to give a more refined taste and to make matching with wine easier, but this does affect the preserving function of the liquid. Be sure to keep these pickles in the fridge so they don't spoil.

PICKLED CAULIFLOWER

Makes: 250ml (8½fl oz) jar

30g (1¼oz) cauliflower florets, about 1cm (½ inch) long
50g (1¾oz/¼ cup) caster (superfine) sugar
150ml (5fl oz/⅔ cup) white wine vinegar
150ml (5fl oz/⅔ cup) water
5g (⅛ oz/1 tsp) sea salt

Put the cauliflower in a large heatproof bowl. Bring the rest of the ingredients to the boil in a small saucepan, then carefully pour over the florets to cover. Leave for at least 1 hour before using. This will keep in an airtight container in the fridge for up to 2 weeks.

PICKLED SHALLOTS

Makes: 250ml (8½fl oz) jar

4 banana shallots
10g (¼oz/1¾ tsp) sea salt
20g (¾oz/1⅔ tbsp) caster (superfine) sugar
30ml (1fl oz/2 tbsp) white wine vinegar
300ml (10fl oz/1¼ cups) water
50ml (2fl oz/scant ¼ cup) extra virgin olive oil

Peel the shallots and slice into rings, keeping the root intact. Put the salt, sugar, vinegar and water into a saucepan and bring to the boil. As soon as it boils, add the shallots and simmer for just 2 minutes, then strain the shallots and discard the liquid. Toss the shallots in the olive oil. This will keep in an airtight container in the fridge for up to 2 weeks.

PICKLED BEETROOT (BEETS)

Makes: 150ml (5fl oz) jar

1 small white or red beetroot (beet))
25g (1oz/2 tbsp) caster (superfine) sugar
25ml (1fl oz/5 tsp) cider or white wine vinegar
50ml (2fl oz/scant ¼ cup) water
2.5g (scant ½ tsp) sea salt

If using a red beetroot (beet), line a chopping board with 4 layers of cling film (plastic wrap) and wear gloves to prevent staining. Peel the beetroot (beet) and cut into the largest cube you can. Cut into 2mm (¹⁄₁₆-inch) slices on a mandolin. Using a sharp knife cut each slice into 2mm (¹⁄₁₆-inch) strips. Then bunching the strips, cut them into 2mm (¹⁄₁₆-inch) cubes. Place the cubes in a small heatproof bowl.

Put the rest of the ingredients into a small saucepan and bring to the boil, then pour over the beetroot (beet). Leave for 2 hours then strain. This will keep in an airtight container in the fridge for up to 2 weeks.

« pickled shallots

pickled carrot »

« pickled pear

« pickled cauliflower

« sauerkraut

pickled beetroot (beets) »

« kimchi

PICKLED CARROTS

Makes: 250–500ml (8½–18fl oz) jar

3 large carrots, peeled and trimmed
25g (1oz/2 tbsp) caster (superfine) sugar
50ml (2fl oz/scant ¼ cup) white wine
50ml (2fl oz/scant ¼ cup) white wine vinegar
75ml (2¾fl oz/⅓ cup) water
3g (½ tsp) sea salt
50ml (2fl oz/scant ¼ cup) extra virgin olive oil
2g thyme sprigs (including stalks)
1 star anise

Using a mandolin, cut the carrots lengthways into ribbons to the thickness of cereal box card. Alternatively, cut the carrot into thin rounds using a sharp knife.

Bring the rest of the ingredients to the boil in a small saucepan, then remove from the heat and add the carrots. Stir well, then set aside to cool in the saucepan.

Once cold, transfer to a jar and store in the fridge for at least 4 hours before using. This will keep in the fridge for 2 weeks.

PICKLED KOHLRABI

Makes: 250ml (8½fl oz) jar

1 kohlrabi, skin removed
30g (1¼oz/2½ tbsp) caster (superfine) sugar
60ml (2¼fl oz/¼ cup) white wine vinegar
90ml (3¼fl oz/generous ⅓ cup) water

Cut the kohlrabi into even 5mm (¼-inch) cubes and put into a heatproof bowl.

Bring the rest of the ingredients to the boil in a small saucepan, then pour over the kohlrabi and leave to cool. Once cold, transfer to a storage jar and store in the fridge for at least 2 hours before using. This will keep for up to 2 weeks in the fridge.

PICKLED PEAR

Makes: 100ml (3½fl oz) jar

1 Williams pear
30g (1¼oz/2½ tbsp) caster (superfine) sugar
60ml (2¼fl oz/¼ cup) white wine vinegar
90ml (3¼fl oz/generous ⅓ cup) water
3g (½ tsp) sea salt

Peel the pear, cut into quarters, remove the core and cut into 7mm (⅓-inch) pieces.

Put the rest of the ingredients into a small saucepan and bring to the boil. Add the diced pear and cook for 20 seconds, then remove from the heat and allow to cool completely before using. This will keep in the fridge for 3 days.

PICKLED CABBAGE

Makes: 500ml–1-litre (17fl oz–1¾-pint) jar

1 small white cabbage
200g (7oz/1 cup) caster (superfine) sugar
400ml (13½fl oz/1⅔ cups) white wine vinegar
800ml (28fl oz/3⅓ cups) water
20g (¾oz/1¼ tbsp) sea salt
4 cloves
4g (2 tsp) caraway seeds

Cut the cabbage into quarters and remove the core. Slice very thinly using a mandolin and put into a large heatproof bowl.

Put the rest of the ingredients into a saucepan and bring to the boil, then immediately pour the liquid over the cabbage. Stir to ensure the cabbage is completely covered, then leave to pickle for at least 4 hours before using. This will keep in an airtight container in the fridge for up to 2 weeks.

SAUERKRAUT

Shop-bought sauerkraut bears almost no resemblance to the real thing. It has been mass produced and pasteurized, which almost completely defeats the point of it. Making it at home is really easy, and once it's made it will keep for months in the fridge.

Makes: 1-litre (1¾-pint) jar

1 large white cabbage, quartered and core removed
sea salt
pinch of caraway seeds (optional)

Sterilize a 1-litre (1¾-pint) glass jar by bringing a large saucepan of water to the boil and submerging the jar and lid in it. Boil for 10 minutes and then carefully remove. Allow to cool and dry.

Slice each cabbage quarter thinly crossways on a mandolin and place in a large, clean bowl. Weigh and calculate 2 per cent of the cabbage weight. Add that amount of salt (for 1kg (2¼lb) of cabbage add 20g (¾oz/1¼ tbsp) of salt).

Mix the cabbage and salt together and leave to stand for 10 minutes. Massage the mix for 2 minutes, then leave for a further 10 minutes. Keep repeating this until the water released covers the cabbage. Add a pinch or 2 of caraway seeds, if you wish, and mix in well. Transfer the cabbage to your prepared jar and then pour enough of the released liquid over the top to cover.

Cut a circle of baking parchment just bigger than the top of the jar and push this down inside the jar to keep the cabbage submerged under the liquid. Place the lid on the jar but do not fasten it. Place it somewhere with a warm, stable temperature (21°C/70°F) for 5 days. Check every day to make sure the water has not overflowed or disappeared.

After 5 days, take out the paper and taste the sauerkraut – it should taste pleasantly fermented. Return the paper to the top, firmly attach the lid and put into the fridge to store.

This will keep for at least 2 months in the fridge.

KIMCHI

Kimchi is sauerkraut's spicy cousin and takes four to five days to mature properly. There are as many recipes as there are people who make it, each with its own charms, but my version is very straightforward as I like to keep my flavours simple and clean.

Makes: 1-litre (1¾-pint) jar

1 small white cabbage, quartered and core removed
6 mild red chillies, cut in half lengthways, seeds discarded, sliced very thinly
4 spring onions (scallions), very finely sliced
2 carrots, peeled and coarsely grated
sea salt

Sterilize a 1-litre (1¾-pint) glass jar (see left). Follow all steps of the Sauerkraut method (left), adding the chillies, spring onions (scallions) and carrots to the sliced cabbage, and weighing the total mix to calculate the salt ratio.

After 5 days, try the kimchi. It should taste pleasantly fermented and a bit moreish. Return the paper to the top, firmly attach the lid and store in the fridge.

This will keep for at least 2 months in the fridge.

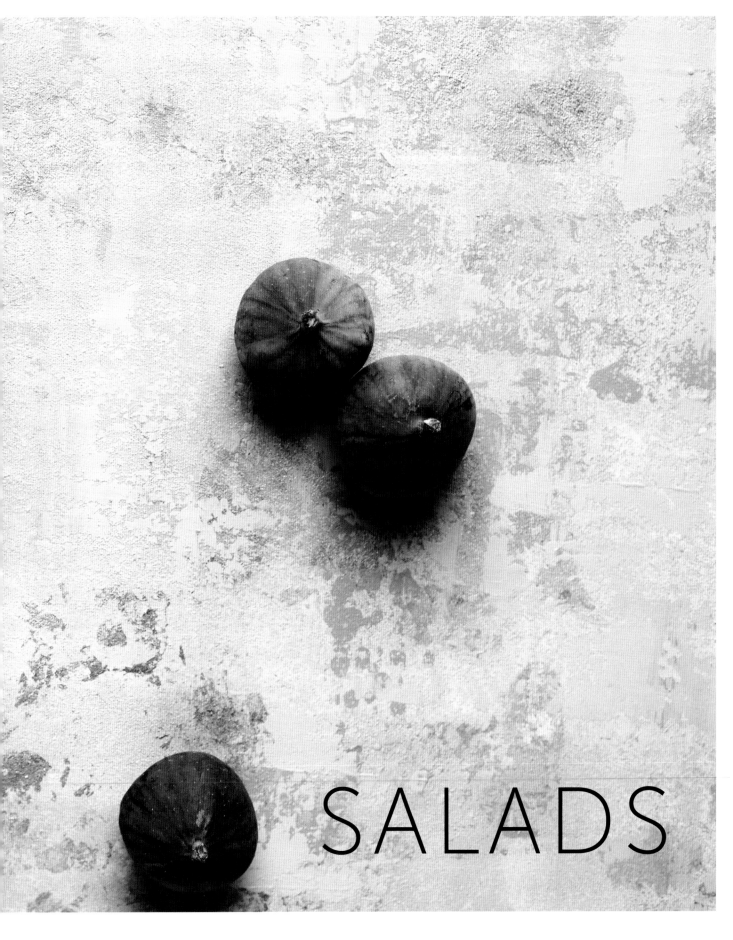

SALADS

I always used to cut fennel lengthways, to show off the shape of the bulb, but it was often a bit stringy as the fibres of the fennel run lengthways along the petals. At some point I realized that cutting fennel across, while not quite as visually satisfying, eliminated this problem. Food is firstly about how good it is to the mouth and only secondly to the eye, so now I cut my raw fennel across instead.

I learnt the technique used on the hazelnuts from Acorn's head chef Steven, and it is a great way to cook nuts, lifting this salad from good to great. It is, however, a lot of work for a scattering of nuts. Should you choose instead to pan-fry your hazelnuts in a little oil until golden, before sprinkling them with a touch of salt, no one would think any less of you, except possibly Steven.

Serves: 4

FENNEL & HAZELNUT SALAD

FOR THE DRESSING
30ml (1fl oz/2 tbsp) hazelnut oil
10ml (2 tsp) lemon juice
3g (½ tsp) sea salt

FOR THE SALAD
1 x quantity of candied hazelnuts
    (see page 116)
2 heads of red chicory (endive)
2 fennel bulbs
10g (¼oz/2⅔ tbsp) flat-leaf parsley
    leaves
10g (¼oz) chervil leaves

Prepare the candied hazelnuts (see page 116).

Mix the hazelnut oil, lemon juice and salt together to make the dressing. Separate out the chicory (endive) bulbs into leaves and cut any that are bigger than the length of your thumb into smaller pieces. Set to one side.

When ready to serve, prepare the fennel. Trim the bottom from the fennel to leave a flat base. Using a mandolin, slice the fennel bulb from the bottom into 1mm slices (very thin but with just enough thickness to retain a crunch). Put the chicory and sliced fennel together in a bowl and add the herb leaves. Mix dry to make sure they are well dispersed, then pour over the dressing and mix again well. Add the nuts, stir through and serve.

This salad goes very well with everyday bread (see page 212) or my green lentil & onion pâté (see page 74).

Good food cannot be rushed. The slow process of developing flavours and complexity is a pleasure in itself, one that is in danger of being lost in a world of 30-minute meals and quick-fix dinners. This salad takes several days to prepare well, but each gentle stage develops texture and flavour layers that simply using canned beans and roasted tomatoes cannot achieve. For me, good food is about using that ultimate and most precious of ingredients, time.

Serves: 4

CONFIT TOMATO SALAD
with white beans and black olives

FOR THE CONFIT TOMATOES
8 top-quality plum tomatoes
6g (1 tsp) sea salt
25ml (1fl oz/5 tsp) sherry vinegar (or red wine vinegar)
4g (⅛oz) thyme leaves
4g (⅛oz) sprigs of tarragon
4 whole cloves of garlic
750ml (26fl oz/3 cups) extra virgin olive oil

FOR THE WHITE BEANS
100g (3½oz/½ cup) dried cannellini beans
1 onion, cut into large chunks
3 sticks of celery, cut into large chunks
1 bay leaf
5g (⅛oz) sprigs of thyme
5g (⅛oz) sprigs of tarragon
10 black peppercorns
1 litre (1¾ pints/4 cups) water
5g (⅛oz/1 tsp) sea salt
10g (¼oz/1 tbsp) flat-leaf parsley leaves, finely chopped

TO SERVE
black olive tapenade (see page 38)
4 sliced black olives
handful of parsley leaves

You will need to prepare the confit tomatoes and soak the cannellini beans 1 day before serving. Remove the stem of each plum tomato, then cut a cross in the skin at the bottom. Blanch the tomatoes in boiling water until the skin starts to split, then shock in ice-cold water (see page 185). Peel off the skins, cut each tomato in half, discard the seeds and place in a large bowl. Add the salt, mix well and leave for 1 hour, then add the vinegar, herbs and garlic and stir well. Leave for at least 1 hour, but ideally overnight.

Put the dried beans in a large bowl and cover with cold water by at least 4cm (1½ inches). Soak for at least 6 hours and ideally overnight. Make the black olive tapenade (see page 38).

Preheat the oven to (fan) 100°C/120°C/240°F/gas mark ¼–½. Remove the tomatoes from the macerating juice (reserving the juice) and lay them face down in a baking tray (sheet) or casserole dish that is just big enough to fit them all in. Pour the olive oil over the tomatoes until they are just covered. Remove the garlic and herbs from the macerating liquid and put them in with the tomatoes. Bake the tomatoes for 30–40 minutes, until cooked but not breaking down. Transfer each tomato carefully to a plate and allow to cool, reserving the oil.

Meanwhile, drain and rinse the soaked beans and put them into a large saucepan with the onion, celery, bay leaf, thyme, tarragon and peppercorns. Add the measured water and gently bring to the boil. Half cover the saucepan with a lid and simmer gently, topping up the water if needed to keep the beans submerged, until they are tender but not broken up (this could take up to 2 hours). Top the water back up, add the salt and cook for 10 more minutes. Drain the beans and remove the onion, celery, herbs and peppercorns. Put the beans into a bowl and measure the macerating liquid from the tomatoes, then add it to the bowl with the beans. Add the same amount of reserved cooking oil and allow the beans to cool in the mix, ideally for several hours. When ready to serve, mix in the parsley.

Spoon the cannellini beans into the bottom of 4 low-sided starter bowls, with enough of the bean liquid dressing for the beans to sit in but not be covered. Arrange 4 tomato halves in each bowl, on top of the beans. Scatter with the sliced olives and parsley leaves and serve with the black olive tapenade. This is also delicious with crusty bread and a fresh green salad.

Serves: 4

PAN-FRIED CAULIFLOWER SALAD
with a caper, pine nut and chilli dressing

For the cauliflower

2 large cauliflowers
20g (¾oz/scant 3 tbsp) gram flour
5g (⅛oz/2 tsp) paprika
60ml (2¼fl oz/¼ cup) extra virgin
   olive oil, for frying

FOR THE DRESSING

40g (1½oz/¼ cup) small capers
   in salt
25g (1oz/3 tbsp) pine nuts
80ml (3fl oz/⅓ cup) extra virgin
   olive oil
2 cloves of garlic, puréed (see page
   147)
2 red chillies (not too hot), cut in
   half, deseeded and finely sliced
zest of 2 lemons
40ml (1½fl oz/8 tsp) lemon juice
20g (¾oz/⅓ cup) parsley leaves,
   finely chopped
20g (¾oz/¾ cup) mint leaves,
   finely sliced
4g (¾ tsp) sea salt

Put 4 litres (7 pints/16 cups) of water and 60g (2oz/3½ tbsp) of salt into a large saucepan and bring to the boil. Separate the cauliflower into florets and peel off any woody skin on the stem. Add the florets to the boiling water and simmer gently for 4–6 minutes until cooked but still al dente (a knife will just pass through the stem). Shock in ice-cold water (see page 185), then drain and pat dry.

Preheat the oven to (fan) 160°C/180°C/350°F/gas mark 4.

Make the dressing. Place the capers in a small bowl and cover with cold water. Drain and re-cover with water, then leave to soak for 1 hour. Put the pine nuts on a small baking tray (sheet) and bake in the oven for 5 minutes. Leave to cool slightly, then crush gently using a pestle and mortar, so they are just broken with some whole pieces. Remove the capers from the water (leaving the salt) and dry on kitchen (paper) towel.

Heat the olive oil in a small saucepan and add the capers. Fry gently until they begin to go crispy, then add the garlic and fry for 30 seconds. Remove from the heat, stir in the chillies and pine nuts and allow to cool. Add the lemon zest and juice, parsley, mint and salt to the saucepan. Mix well.

Mix the gram flour and paprika together in a small bowl. Lightly sprinkle it over the cauliflower florets, making sure there is a light coating with no lumps, then rub it on. Turn the cauliflower over and do the same on the other side. Heat the olive oil in a large, wide-based frying pan (skillet), place the cauliflower in the pan and fry until a deep golden brown. Turn over and repeat on the other side. You may need to cook it in batches, adding more oil if necessary, keeping the cooked cauliflower warm.

Serve the cauliflower with the dressing drizzled generously over the top.

Cylindra beetroots (beets) are a long, dark red variety with a flavour profile identical to the round dark red varieties. Their main advantage is they are an even width down most of their length, so when you slice them all of your slices are the same size. If you can only find the round variety then cut them into wedges as this is a better way of ensuring they cook at the same speed.

Serves: 4

ROASTED CYLINDRA BEETROOT (BEETS)
with crushed blackberry dressing and pistachio purée

FOR THE ROASTED BEETROOT (BEETS)
2 large cylindra beetroot (beets)
10g (¼oz) sprigs of thyme
1g (a pinch) dried lavender
5g (⅛oz/1 tsp) sea salt
50ml (2fl oz/scant ¼ cup) water
25ml (1fl oz/5 tsp) extra virgin
    olive oil

FOR THE DRESSING
40ml (1½fl oz/8 tsp) thyme oil (see
    page 220)
100g (3½oz/⅔ cup) blackberries,
    quartered
5ml (1 tsp) red wine vinegar
3g (⅔ tsp) caster (superfine) sugar
pinch of sea salt

FOR THE PURÉE
100g (3½oz/¾ cup) Iranian
    pistachios
100ml (3½fl oz/scant ½ cup) extra
    virgin olive oil
150ml (5fl oz/⅔ cup) water
1 clove of garlic
sea salt
pinch of cayenne pepper

FOR THE GARNISH
10g (¼oz/generous 1 tbsp) Iranian
    pistachios, cut into large chunks
2 sprigs of thyme, leaves picked
20 small red mustard frill leaves

You need to make the thyme oil at least a day, and preferably up to 2 weeks, in advance (see page 220).

Preheat the oven to (fan) 140°C/160°C/310°F/gas mark 2½. Place a 45cm (18-inch) strip of foil over a deep baking tray (sheet) and cover with a 45cm (18-inch) strip of baking parchment, forming a well in the middle. Put the beetroot (beets) and the rest of the beetroot (beet) ingredients into the well and mix together. Fold the tin foil/paper in half and roll up the edges to form a sealed parcel. Bake for 1–2 hours.

About 30 minutes before the beetroot (beets) are cooked, make the blackberry dressing. Put the blackberries in a small bowl and add the vinegar, sugar and salt. Gently crush the blackberries with the back of a fork to break them up but do not reduce them to a purée. Leave to macerate for 20 minutes, then stir in the thyme oil and set aside.

Next make the pistachio purée. Blend the pistachios, olive oil, water and garlic in a blender until silky smooth. Season with salt and a pinch of cayenne pepper (see page 15). Set aside.

After 1–2 hours of cooking test the beetroot (beets) – they should be meltingly soft. If not ready, cook for a little longer then re-test. When ready, allow to cool a little and then rub the skin from the beetroot. Cut them into 1cm (½-inch) slices.

Place 2 tablespoons of pistachio purée on each of 4 starter-sized plates and allow it to run out to make a round pool. Place 2–3 slices of the warm beetroot (beets) across each other next to the purée, and scoop some of the blackberry dressing over the top. Scatter with the chopped pistachios and thyme leaves. Toss the mustard frill leaves in the remaining liquid from the blackberries and arrange on the plates. Serve warm.

Figs have a wonderful, complex sweetness and are perfect partners to red wine, bitter leaves and, surprisingly, curry. This salad plays with a few different flavour partners and, as is often the case with flavours that revolve around a central ingredient, finds a harmony and balance between them. Enjoy this salad with crusty bread and a glass of heavy red wine.

Serves: 4

RED WINE POACHED FIGS
with candied curried pecans and pickled shallots

FOR THE POACHED FIGS
450ml (16fl oz/scant 2 cups)
    red wine
40g (1½oz/¼ cup) brown sugar
2 cloves
1 bay leaf
6 sprigs of thyme
6g (⅛oz/1 tsp) sea salt
10 figs

FOR THE SALAD
curried candied pecans (see
    page 117)
pickled shallots (see page 98)
fig chutney (see page 38)
fresh winter salad leaves, such
    as watercress and red chicory
    (endive)
2 fresh figs, thinly sliced

Make the curried candied pecans (see page 117), pickled shallots (see page 98) and fig chutney (see page 38).

Preheat the oven to (fan) 160°C/180°C/350°F/gas mark 4. Put all the poaching ingredients, except the figs, into a small saucepan and bring to the boil.

Cut the figs in half lengthways and place cut side down on a deep baking tray (sheet). Pour the boiling wine over them, then place in the oven. Cook for 20–30 minutes, shaking gently every 10 minutes to make sure they remain moist. Check after 20 minutes – they should have softened a little but still hold their shape. When cooked, remove from the oven and allow to cool.

Pour the wine from the figs back into the saucepan and simmer gently until it reduces to a syrup. Pour the red wine reduction back over the figs.

Arrange a handful of salad leaves and the fresh fig slices on each plate. Split the poached fig halves between each plate and drizzle the red wine reduction over the top. Scatter several curried candied pecans on each plate and add rounds of pickled shallot. Put a scoop of fig chutney on the side and serve with crusty bread if you wish.

MIXED TOASTED SEEDS

This makes enough for about 10 meals, although you can easily just eat them all without really meaning to straight from the oven – they're very moreish.

Makes: 1 small jar

20g (¾oz/2½ tbsp) sunflower seeds
5g (⅛oz/½ tbsp) poppy seeds
10g (¼oz/4 tsp) sesame seeds
10g (¼oz/1 tbsp) flax seeds
10g (¼oz/4 tsp) hemp seeds
½ tsp extra virgin olive oil
1g (scant ¼ tsp) sea salt, finely ground

Preheat the oven to (fan) 160°C/180°C/350°F/gas mark 4. Mix all the seeds together with the oil on a baking tray (sheet) and roast for 5 minutes until just golden. Sprinkle with the salt and allow to cool.

These can be kept in an airtight container for up to 2 weeks.

ROASTED CHICKPEAS (GARBANZO BEANS)

If you use a lot of aquafaba (see page 76), then you'll end up with a lot of chickpeas (garbanzo beans). Roasting them makes them a great texture for salads or soups, and they will keep for longer.

Makes: 1 small jar

50g (1¾oz/⅓ cup) chickpeas (garbanzo beans)
10ml (2 tsp) extra virgin olive oil
0.5g (¼ tsp) fennel seeds
large pinch of sea salt

Preheat the oven to (fan) 160°C/180°C/350°F/gas mark 4.

Mix all the ingredients together and put onto a small baking tray (sheet). Bake in the oven for 15 minutes until crisp and golden, mixing every 5 minutes.

Remove from the oven and drain on kitchen (paper) towel. Leave to cool, then place on a board and crush with the side of a large knife.

This will keep for up to 3 days in an airtight container.

SEEDED FREEKEH

Freekeh is a little like couscous, but made from toasted wheat. Using toasted seeds in this mix helps to emphasize its nutty character and makes it deliciously moreish.

Serves: 4

300g (10½oz/2 cups) freekeh
10ml (2 tsp) extra virgin olive oil
60g (2oz/scant ½ cup) sunflower seeds
30g (1¼oz/scant ¼ cup) pumpkin seeds
10g (¼oz/4 tsp) sesame seeds

Bring 3 litres (5¼ pints/12½ cups) of water and 30g (1¼oz/1¾ tbsp) of salt to the boil in a large saucepan. Add the freekeh and boil for 10–15 minutes until soft then drain.

Put the oil into a large frying pan (skillet) and add the sunflower seeds and pumpkin seeds. Heat the pan and gently fry the seeds until they pop and become golden then add the sesame seeds and stir. Add the cooked freekeh and stir to mix the seeds through the freekeh.

This is best eaten straight away.

PISTACHIO DUKKAH

Dukkah is a blend of nuts and spices used as a garnish in the Middle East. This uses pistachios, because they have a more buttery texture than most nuts.

Makes: 1 small jar

10g (¼oz/1¾ tbsp) coriander seeds
2.5g (1¼ tsp) cumin seeds
5g (⅛oz/1 tsp) sea salt
15g (½oz/2 tbsp) sesame seeds
50g (1¾oz/⅓ cup) Iranian pistachios

Preheat the oven to (fan) 160°C/180°C/350°F/gas mark 4. Toast the coriander seeds and cumin seeds together in a hot frying pan (skillet) until fragrant. Using a pestle and mortar, grind the coriander seeds, cumin seeds and salt to a coarse sandy texture. Transfer to a bowl.

On 2 baking trays (sheets) roast the sesame seeds and pistachios separately in the oven for 4 minutes, then leave to cool. Use the pestle and mortar to grind the sesame seeds to break them up, then transfer to the bowl with the spices. Crush the pistachios using the pestle and mortar to form crumbs. Add to the spices in the bowl and mix to combine.

This will keep for up to 1 month in an airtight container.

BLACK OLIVE CRUMBS

Something wonderful happens when you dry olives out – they become salty, intense and delicious. These black olive crumbs are great with any dish that needs a salty bitter edge.

Makes: 2 tablespoons

50g (1¾oz/⅓ cup) good-quality pitted black kalamata olives

Ideally use a dehydrator set to 45°C/113°F or preheat the oven to its lowest setting.

Spread the olives out on a dehydrator tray and dehydrate for 6 hours or until very dry and crispy. If using the oven, spread on a baking tray (sheet) and check every hour, turning them over, and cook for 6 hours. Chop into crumbs.

This will keep in an airtight container for up to 2 weeks.

CANDIED FENNEL SEEDS

These are great sprinkled over desserts, but are equally good as a little spattering of interest over salads or soups. If you are lucky enough to grow fennel, let a few bulbs run to seed and harvest them for the freshest, cleanest taste you can imagine.

Makes: 80g (3oz)

60g (2oz/⅓ cup) caster (superfine) sugar
30ml (1fl oz/2 tbsp) water
60g (2oz/⅔ cup) fennel seeds

Put the sugar and water in a small, heavy-based saucepan and heat to 137°C/278°F. Remove from the heat and add the fennel seeds. Stir hard until the sugar crystallizes and the fennel seeds separate from each other.

These will keep in an airtight container for up to 3 months.

SMOKED NUTS

Smoke and nuts is a fantastic modern flavour. Use these to bring a wonderful interest to any plate.

Makes: 100g (3½oz)

100g (3½oz/¾ cup) blanched hazelnuts, almonds
  or cashew nuts

Put 1 tablespoon of hickory chips into a stove-top smoker. Line the top grate with foil to prevent the nuts from escaping and follow the manufacturer's instructions.

Smoke the nuts until they have a pronounced smoky flavour. Remove from the smoker and leave to cool.

These will keep for 2 weeks in an airtight container.

CANDIED HAZELNUTS OR ALMONDS

This is a great way of preparing nuts to add not only a nutty edge but also a little sweetness to a dish.

Makes: 100g (3½ oz)

100g (3½oz/½ cup) caster (superfine) sugar
100ml (3½fl oz/scant ½ cup) water
50g (1¾oz/⅓ cup) blanched hazelnuts or almonds
neutral oil, for deep-fat frying

Prepare your deep-fat fryer (see page 26).

Put all the ingredients into a small saucepan and bring to the boil. Simmer gently until the water reaches 110°C/230°F and then strain the nuts from the liquid.

Add the nuts to the deep-fat fryer and fry for about 2 minutes until a light golden colour. Remove the nuts from the oil and transfer to a baking tray (sheet) or plate (do not line it with kitchen (paper) towel as the nuts will stick). Leave to cool.

These will keep in an airtight container for up to 1 month.

IMPROVISED SMOKER

If you don't have a stove-top smoker, you can improvise using a steamer basket. Put a piece of foil on the base of the steamer saucepan to prevent the chips from discolouring it. Put the smoking chips on to the foil and heat the saucepan on a medium–high heat until the chips burn. (If they don't burn, then use a blowtorch, lighter or match.) Once they are burning well, put on the steamer basket (containing the ingredients intended to smoke) and then put on the lid. Turn down the heat to medium and leave for 10–15 minutes until the desired level of smokiness is achieved.

CURRIED CANDIED PECANS

These are one of my favourite things in the world. I struggle to stop eating them, and only knowing the price of pecans slows me down.

Makes: 120g (4¼oz)

100g (3½oz/scant 1 cup) pecan nuts
10g (¼oz/1⅔ tbsp) mild Madras curry powder
2g (⅓ tsp) sea salt
100g (3½oz/½ cup) caster (superfine) sugar
30ml (1fl oz/2 tbsp) water

Preheat the oven to (fan) 160°C/180°C/350°F/gas mark 4. Put the pecan nuts on a baking tray (sheet) and roast for 8 minutes, then set aside to cool.

Mix the curry powder and salt with the pecans in a small bowl.

Put the sugar in a small, heavy-based saucepan with the water and heat gently until it reaches 137°C/278°F. Remove immediately from the heat and add the pecans, stirring very hard until the sugar crystallizes and the pecans separate from each other. Leave to cool.

These will keep for 3 months in an airtight container.

CURRIED POPCORN

If you're cooking with sweetcorn and you need to add a bit of texture, it seems silly not to use popcorn. This version adds curry flavours, but fresh rosemary, chilli and black pepper are also fantastic with popcorn.

Makes: 2 cups

2g (1 tsp) mild Madras curry powder
1g (scant ¼ tsp) sea salt
10ml (2 tsp) rapeseed oil
30g (1¼oz/⅛ cup) popcorn kernels

Using a pestle and mortar, grind the curry powder and salt to a powder.

Put the oil into a heavy-based lidded saucepan along with 2 popcorn kernels. Heat the oil with the lid on until the 2 kernels pop, then remove them and add the remaining kernels. Stir to coat them all in oil. Put the lid on and shake the saucepan constantly. The kernels should begin to pop frantically.

Once the popping slows to every 3 seconds, remove the saucepan from the heat and sprinkle in your curry powder mix.

This will keep for 3 days in an airtight container.

A NOTE ON CURRY POWDER

As a general rule I hate using pre-made anything, preferring the fresh flavour, control and craftman's satisfaction you get from creating everything from scratch. However, the one thing that has defeated me is Madras curry powder – I never seem to be able to recreate the magical harmony of spices you get from a good-quality shop-bought mix. Each brand has its own blend of spices, but any good-quality brand should deliver the necessary complexity. Just make sure it is a mild mix, as anything spicy will throw a whole new element into the mix.

CABBAGE POWDER

Sometimes you want to add a deep, cooked cabbage note to a dish without the complication or texture of cooked leaves. This powder achieves that and also adds a great visual texture to a plate. As you use it sparingly, this will make enough for about 20 servings.

Makes: 1–2 tbsp

200g (7oz) dark green spring green or cabbage leaves

Ideally use a dehydrator set to 45°C/113°F, or preheat the oven to its lowest setting.

Put 4 litres (7 pints/16 cups) of water and 40g (1½oz/ 2½ tbsp) of salt into a large saucepan and bring to the boil. Blanch the cabbage leaves for 1 minute and shock in ice-cold water (see page 185).

Spread the cabbage out on a dehydrator tray and dehydrate for 8 hours or until very dry and crispy. If using the oven, spread out on a baking tray (sheet) and cook for 6–8 hours.

Using a spice grinder or pestle and mortar, grind the dried leaves to a fine powder. This will keep in a jar for 2 weeks.

ONION POWDER

You can buy onion powder, but it is never as fresh and sweet as when you make it yourself.

Makes: 100g (3½oz)

4 brown-skinned onions, peeled and sliced

Ideally use a dehydrator set to 45°C/113°F, or preheat the oven to its lowest setting.

Spread the onion slices out on a dehydrator tray and dehydrate for 4 hours until dry and crispy, with a little colour. If using the oven, spread out on a baking tray (sheet) and cook for 6–8 hours.

Using a pestle and mortar grind the onions into a fine powder. This will keep in an airtight container for up to 2 months.

PORCINI POWDER

This will make a lot of powder, but you will find that it is easier to blend large quantities and there are numerous uses for it once you have it to hand. If you are lucky enough to have an electric coffee grinder then blend what you need, when you need it, to guarantee a fresh bright flavour.

Makes: 90g (3oz)

100g (3½oz) dried porcini mushrooms

Put the porcinis into a blender or spice grinder and blend to a fine powder.

This will keep in a sealed jar for months.

ORANGE ZEST POWDER

This adds citrus notes, a splash of colour and interest to any dish so it's well worth having a jar in your cupboard. Although this only makes a couple of tablespoons that is enough for about 20 servings.

Makes: 1–2 tablespoons

4 organic, unwaxed oranges

Ideally use a dehydrator set to 45°C/113°F, or preheat the oven to its lowest setting.

Peel the zest from the orange in strips, avoiding as much of the white pith as you can. Put the strips onto a dehydrator tray and dehydrate for 8 hours or until completely dry and brittle. If using the oven, place on a baking tray (sheet) and dry out for 2 hours, then check.

Using a pestle and mortar, grind the dried strips into a fine powder.

This will keep for 2 weeks in an airtight container.

ORANGE ZAATAR MIX

Zaatar traditionally uses sumac powder to bring acidity and colour to the mix. Substituting this for orange zest powder (see left) tones down the acidity, replacing it with an astringency and brings more citrus notes, making it great for adding aromas to a dish without upsetting the acidity balance. This makes enough for four servings.

Makes: 2 tablespoons

15g (½oz/2 tbsp) sesame seeds
5g (⅛oz/2½ tsp) cumin seeds
3g (½ tbsp) fennel seeds
5g (⅛oz) orange zest powder (see left)

Preheat the oven to (fan) 160°C/180°C/350°F/gas mark 4. Put the sesame seeds on a small baking tray (sheet) and toast in the oven for 5 minutes.

Mix the cumin and fennel seeds together, place on a small baking tray (sheet), and toast in the oven for 5 minutes. Leave to cool, then grind the cumin and fennel seeds to a coarse sand texture using a pestle and mortar.

Mix all the ingredients together. This will keep for 2 weeks in an airtight container.

MAINS

Making cavatelli is a great way into homemade pasta. Because they are quite thick, you can use a variety of doughs, greatly extending the flavouring options. Setting aside their relative ease, they are also a great-shaped pasta, they have a real bite and their density means the flavour of the dough can easily be detected.

Serves: 4

PORCINI CAVATELLI
with asparagus and a white wine and mushroom sauce

FOR THE CAVATELLI

20g (¾oz) porcini powder (see page 118)

400g (14oz/2⅓ cups) semolina, plus extra to dust

170ml (6fl oz/⅔ cup) water

20ml (4 tsp) extra virgin olive oil

FOR THE WHITE WINE SAUCE

1 litre (1¾ pints/4 cups) mushroom stock (see page 65)

25ml (1fl oz/5 tsp) extra virgin olive oil

1 banana shallot, finely diced

250ml (8½fl oz/1 cup) dry white wine

100g (3½oz) pine nut butter (see page 221)

sea salt

FOR THE ASPARAGUS

4 tbsp asparagus & herb purée (see page 182)

21 asparagus spears, trimmed and peeled

25ml (1fl oz/5 tsp) truffle oil

Make the porcini powder (see page 118), pine nut butter (see page 221), asparagus & herb purée (see page 182) and mushroom stock (see page 65) in advance. Remove the purée from the fridge to come to room temperature.

Mix the porcini powder and semolina in a bowl. Add the water and then the olive oil. Using a spoon, bring the pasta mix together to form a rough dough, then transfer to a clean, dry work surface. Knead the dough for about 8 minutes, until smooth and supple. Wrap in cling film (plastic wrap) and put in the fridge for 30 minutes to rest, and ideally for longer as it will get firmer and easier to work with. It will keep for up to 3 days in the fridge, just remove from the fridge 30 minutes before using.

Make the cavatelli (see shaping cavatelli, page 127).

Make the white wine and mushroom sauce. Put the mushroom stock into a small saucepan and simmer gently until it has reduced by half, then remove from the heat.

When the mushroom stock has been simmering for 10 minutes, heat the olive oil in a large frying pan (skillet) and add the shallot. Fry gently for about 2 minutes, until softened but not coloured, then add the white wine. Cook to reduce the wine by three-quarters, then add the mushroom stock reduction. Continue simmering until it has reduced by half, then add the pine nut butter, whisking it in until emulsified. You should have a rich, thick sauce. If it is a little thin, simmer gently until it reaches the correct consistency. Season with salt to taste (see page 15).

While the sauce is cooking, cook the cavatelli (see cooking pasta, page 127) and the asparagus spears. Put 4 litres (7 pints/16 cups) of water into a large saucepan, add 60g (2oz/3½ tbsp) of salt and bring to the boil. Add 20 of the asparagus spears, keeping one spear raw, and cook for 2–3 minutes until just over al dente but still a vibrant green colour. Remove immediately and put into a bowl. Add the truffle oil, toss well to coat all the spears and keep warm by laying a clean tea towel over the top.

Once the sauce is cooked add the cavatelli and heat gently until the sauce has a beautiful consistency, like that of double cream.

Peel the raw asparagus spear lengthways into strips using a vegetable peeler. Drizzle 2 tablespoons of asparagus purée around the edge of each of 4 large plates, then add the cavatelli, in its sauce. Arrange 5 spears of asparagus on each plate, and top with the asparagus strips. Drizzle the plate generously with truffle oil and serve hot.

This dish is all about the fresh green colour and flavour – the quality of your ingredients and the craft of your pasta work should have the space to sing. Use the freshest beans you can find, the most vibrant basil, and take your time making the perfect trofie. Use this recipe as a guide to how many beans you will need (include the same amount of beans as trofie), just use an abundance of different kinds to make this a true celebration of the season.

Serves: 4

SPINACH TROFIE
with summer beans and pesto

FOR THE TROFIE
125g (4½oz/4 cups) spinach
75ml (2¾fl oz/⅓ cup) water
300g (10½oz/1¾ cups) fine yellow semolina, plus extra to dust
15ml (1 tbsp) extra virgin olive oil

FOR THE BEANS
100g (3½oz) fine green (string) beans
100g (3½oz) podded broad (fava) beans
100g (3½oz) runner beans
100g (3½oz) fine asparagus

FOR THE PESTO SAUCE
150g (5½oz) pesto (see page 40)
50ml (2fl oz/scant ¼ cup) water
50ml (2fl oz/scant ¼ cup) extra virgin olive oil

FOR THE GARNISH
20g (¾oz/2½ tbsp) pine nuts
10g (¼oz/⅓ cup) small basil leaves (or large leaves, shredded)
black pepper
extra virgin olive oil

First make the pesto (see page 40). Next make the spinach trofie. Blanch the spinach for 30 seconds, until wilted and a vibrant green, then shock in ice-cold water (see page 185). Once cold, collect it into a ball, squeezing out all the water. Roughly chop the ball and place in a blender. Add the measured water and blend to a very smooth purée, with no flecks of green in it.

Measure 140g (5oz) of the spinach purée into a large bowl and add the semolina and olive oil. Using a spoon, bring the pasta mix together to form a rough dough, then transfer to a clean, dry work surface. Knead the dough for about 8 minutes, until smooth and supple. Wrap in cling film (plastic wrap) and put in the fridge for 30 minutes to rest, and ideally for longer as it will get firmer and easier to work with. It will keep for up to 3 days in the fridge, just remove from the fridge 30 minutes before using.

Preheat the oven to (fan) 160°C/180°C/350°F/gas mark 4. Put the pine nuts for the garnish on a small baking tray (sheet) and toast in the oven for 4 minutes. Remove and allow to cool.

Make the spinach trofie (see Shaping Trofie, page 127).

Prepare each type of bean and the asparagus, removing any woody stalks or strings. Blanch the beans and asparagus until al dente (between 30 seconds and 2 minutes depending on the bean), one type of bean at a time to make sure each type is perfectly cooked, then shock in ice-cold water (see page 185). You want them to have a fresh crunch. Cook the trofie (see cooking pasta, page 127).

Put the water and olive oil for the pesto sauce into a large saucepan and bring to the boil. Add the trofie and heat for 30 seconds. Add the beans and heat until everything is just hot. Add the pesto and stir so that it coats everything.

Split the mix between 4 pasta bowls or plates and scatter with the toasted pine nuts, basil, a generous twist of black pepper and a drizzle of olive oil. Serve hot.

| MAKING PASTA |

ROLLING OUT PASTA USING A PASTA MACHINE

Knead the made pasta briefly, then form it into a ball and divide into 4 to 6 pieces. Form the first piece into a rough rectangle then, using a rolling pin, roll into a rectangle about 1cm (½ inch) narrower than the width of your pasta machine.

Set the machine to its widest setting and feed the pasta through. Fold it in half lengthways and feed it back through, it should now be a neat rectangle the same width as the machine.

Reduce the machine thickness by one setting and feed the pasta through again. Continue this process, dusting it with semolina when necessary, until you reach the thickness you want. Repeat with the rest of the pieces of dough.

MAKING PAPPARDELLE

Roll out the pasta using a pasta machine (see above) until the third to last thickness on the machine.

Dust your work surface with semolina and lay the pasta out. Dust well with semolina. Using a fluted pasta roller (or knife) cut the pasta into 2.5cm (1-inch) wide strips across the width of the pasta.

SHAPING TORTELLINI

Roll out the pasta using a pasta machine (see left) until the second to last thickness on the machine.

Dust your work surface with semolina and lay the pasta out. Using a cutter the same size as the width of your pasta sheet (up to 15cm/6 inches), cut as many rounds from it as you can.

Line a baking tray (sheet) with cling film (plastic wrap) and lightly oil it. Mix together 50g (1¾oz/generous ⅓ cup) of plain (all-purpose) flour and 100ml (3½fl oz/scant ½ cup) of water into a paste in a small bowl and set aside.

Pipe or spoon 1 small tablespoon of the filling into the centre of each round. Getting the right amount of filling is critical – too little and the pasta is disappointingly empty; too much, and it will burst open.

Using your finger, spread the flour and water mix onto one half of each pasta round to act as a glue and then fold each round over into a half-moon shape, encapsulating the filling in a neat bulge in the middle.

Using the soft pad of your thumb or finger, carefully but firmly press the pasta down to stick, pushing all the air out of the middle as you do so. You are trying to do 3 things: shape the filling into a neat bubble surrounded by pasta, eliminate any air pockets from the centre, and stick the 2 halves of pasta together. Once you have sealed all the parcels, take the cutter you used earlier and, using a rolling motion, trim the rough edge from your half-moon shape.

Now the tricky part. Dab one corner of the moon liberally with the flour paste and then, using your thumb to form a little crease in the filling bubble, fold both corners toward the middle sticking one to the other and pressing firmly.

Place each finished tortellini on the oiled tray, cover with cling film (plastic wrap) and pop in the fridge for up to 8 hours until needed.

SHAPING CAVATELLI

(See page 122)

Lightly dust your work surface with semolina. Cut the pasta dough into 8 equal pieces. Roll each piece into a sausage 7mm (⅓ inch) thick and cut each sausage into 1.5cm (½-inch) lengths.

Using a pasta board, butter pat or fork take each piece of dough and, using your thumb, in one smooth motion press and roll the dough down the board to flatten it and roll it into a shell-like shape, a little like gnocchi (see page 138). It may take a few attempts to get this right, but persevere as it will be worth it.

SHAPING TROFIE

(See page 125)

Line a baking tray (sheet) with baking parchment and dust with a little semolina. Cut the pasta into 8 equal pieces and roll out each piece into a 5mm (¼-inch) thick sausage.

Cut the sausage into 1cm (½-inch) lengths. Roll each piece into a long, torpedo shape between the palms of your hand.

Set a blunt knife at a 45 degree angle in your hand and set this at 45 degrees to the pasta. Put the knife on the right-hand end of the pasta and pull the knife towards you, pulling the pasta with it and drawing it across to twist the pasta (this is easier than it sounds).

Develop a rhythm and work through the pile as quickly as you can. Dust lightly with semolina and transfer to the prepared baking tray (sheet).

COOKING PASTA

Fill a large saucepan with 6 litres (10 pints/25 cups) of water, add 60g (2oz/3½ tbsp) of salt and bring to the boil.

Using a dough knife or spatula, scoop the pasta into the boiling water. If the water stops boiling, don't add more pasta, just finish the batch already cooking before adding more.

When the pasta floats to the surface allow it to cook for 2 minutes for cavatelli, 1–2 minures for trofie and 5 seconds for pappardelle until al dente. Remove one to test – it should be firm but cooked through. When cooked, remove the pasta with a spider or slotted spoon.

I love this pasta recipe as the gram flour adds a sweet nuttiness and a real bite. If you don't want to go to the effort of making all the components, then just make the pasta and the courgette (zucchini) mix and combine them in a saucepan before serving. It's not as pretty, but it is just as tasty.

Serves: 4

FENNEL SEED PAPPARDELLE

with courgettes (zucchini), chickpeas (garbanzo beans), basil and lemon

FOR THE PAPPARDELLE

0.1g (pinch) saffron
1.5g (¾ tsp) fennel seeds
160ml (5½fl oz/⅔ cup) boiling water
350g (12oz/2 cups) fine semolina,
    plus extra to dust
50g (1¾oz/scant ½ cup) gram flour
15ml (1 tbsp) extra virgin olive oil,
    plus extra to drizzle

FOR THE GRIDDLED COURGETTES (ZUCCHINI)

2 large courgettes (zucchini)
sea salt
extra virgin olive oil

FOR THE COURGETTE (ZUCCHINI) MIX

3 large courgettes (zucchini)
80g (2¾oz/½ cup) canned
    chickpeas (garbanzo beans),
    drained and rinsed
3g (½ tsp) sea salt
50ml (2fl oz/scant ¼ cup) water
75ml (2¾fl oz/⅓ cup) extra virgin
    olive oil
1 dried chilli
1 clove of garlic, puréed (see
    page 147)
zest of ½ lemon
25ml (1fl oz/5 tsp) lemon juice
20g (¾oz/generous ¾ cup) basil
    leaves, shredded

FOR THE GARNISH

roasted chickpeas (garbanzo beans)
    (see page 114)
1 lemon
10g (¼oz/ ⅓ cup) basil leaves
chilli flakes (crushed chilli)

Make the roasted chickpea (garbanzo bean) garnish (see page 114). To make the pappardelle, grind the saffron and fennel seeds to a fine powder using a pestle and mortar. Add the boiling water and leave to infuse for 20 minutes. Put the semolina and gram flour into a large bowl, add the olive oil and measure in the saffron water, first weighing it and making it up to 160g (5¾oz) with cold water. Using a spoon, bring the pasta mix together to form a rough dough, then transfer to a clean, dry work surface. Knead the dough for about 8 minutes, until smooth and supple. Wrap in cling film (plastic wrap) and put in the fridge for 30 minutes, then make the pasta (see making pappardelle, page 126).

Cut the courgettes (zucchini) for the griddled courgettes (zucchini) lengthways into thin strips (about 3mm/⅛ inch) on a mandolin. Weigh, add 1 per cent of their weight in salt, mix well and leave for 30 minutes. Meanwhile, make the courgette (zucchini) mix. Put 4 litres (7 pints/16 cups) of water into a large saucepan with 40g (1½oz/ 2½ tbsp) of salt and bring to the boil. Add the whole courgettes (zucchini) and cook for 10–15 minutes, until soft, then remove to a colander to cool. Put the chickpeas (garbanzo beans), salt, water, 50ml (2fl oz/scant ¼ cup) of olive oil and the dried chilli into a small saucepan and cook gently until the water has just evaporated. Add the garlic, then remove from the heat and set aside.

When the boiled courgettes (zucchini) are cool, cut off and discard the top and bottom and cut into 7mm (⅓ inch) dice. Return to the colander, then using a small plate push down to remove any liquid. Transfer the courgette (zucchini) to a large bowl, and add the hot chickpea (garbanzo bean) mix, lemon zest, lemon juice, basil and the rest of the olive oil. Stir well.

Rinse the courgette (zucchini) slices and dry with kitchen (paper) towel. Heat a griddle pan until very hot and brush the slices with oil. Char, in batches if necessary, on the griddle pan until black ridges appear on one side. Turn over and repeat on the other side. Once cooked, roll up, transfer to a bowl and add a drizzle of olive oil.

Cook the pappardelle in 2 batches (see cooking pasta, page 127). Cook one batch, then put them on a tray lined with non-stick baking parchment. Drizzle with a little olive oil and flatten them out to prevent them sticking. Cover lightly with a clean tea towel and repeat with the rest. Arrange a quarter of the pappardelle on each of 4 large plates. Arrange spoonfuls of the courgette (zucchini) mix and the rolled griddled courgette around the plate and over the pappardelle. Grate a little lemon zest over and sprinkle whole and shredded basil, chilli flakes (crushed chilli) and roasted chickpea (garbanzo) crumble over the top, then serve.

This dish has some big flavours, but the balance is delicate and refined. To make this really well you must remember a few basic principles: the most important of which is that your filling must be firm. If your filling is wet, it will make the tortellini hard to shape and they will go soggy and split. I have suggested adding a little water to the potato mix, but I do so with extreme caution, as I would rather have a coarse filling than a wet mix. Your pasta must also be delicate, and you need to make the filling a day in advance, which means you need to soak the walnuts two days in advance of eating.

Serves: 4

WALNUT TORTELLINI
with a red wine mushroom reduction

FOR THE WALNUT FILLING

200g (7oz/2 cups) walnuts

400g (14oz) whole new potatoes, skin on

30ml (1 fl oz/2 tbsp) walnut oil

50ml (2fl oz/scant ¼ cup) water (if needed)

2.5g (1 tbsp) chopped dill

tiny pinch of cayenne pepper

FOR THE TORTELLINI

0.3g (scant ½ tsp) saffron

175ml (6fl oz/¾ cup) boiling water

400g (14oz/2⅓ cups) fine semolina, plus extra to dust

15ml (1 tbsp) extra virgin olive oil

FOR THE RED WINE REDUCTION

1 litre (1¾ pints/4 cups) mushroom stock (see page 65)

200ml (7fl oz/generous ¾ cup) red wine

1 bay leaf

Put the walnuts in a small bowl and cover with cold water by at least 2cm (¾ inch). Put into the fridge for at least 8 hours or overnight. Prepare the cavolo nero crisps (see page 28) and mushroom stock (see page 65).

Put the potatoes for the filling into a small saucepan with 1 litre (1¾ pints/4 cups) of water and 10g (¼oz/1¾ tsp) of salt and gently bring to the boil, covered with a lid. Simmer gently until the potatoes are soft, then drain.

While the potatoes are still hot, drain and rinse the walnuts. Put the walnuts into a blender and blend until as fine as possible. Transfer the walnuts to a large bowl and add the warm potatoes (with their skins on) and the walnut oil. Mash well, then return to the blender and process until a smooth, creamy texture, adding a little water if necessary. Be careful though, you need a firm mix. When smooth, transfer to a bowl and stir in the dill. Add a tiny pinch of cayenne pepper and check and adjust the seasoning (see page 15). Transfer to a piping bag or small container and put in the fridge for at least 4 hours to firm up.

Make the pasta. Grind the saffron to a fine powder using a pestle and mortar, then add the boiling water and leave to infuse for 20 minutes. Once the saffron is ready, put the semolina into a large bowl, add the olive oil and measure in the saffron water, making it back up to 175ml (6fl oz/¾ cup) with cold water. Using a spoon, bring the pasta mix together to form a rough dough, then transfer to a clean, dry work surface. Knead the dough for about 8 minutes, until smooth and supple. Wrap in cling film (plastic wrap) and put in the fridge for 30 minutes to rest, and ideally for longer as it will get firmer and easier to work with. It will keep for up to 3 days in the fridge, just remove from the fridge 30 minutes before using.

Make the tortellini (see shaping tortellini on page 126).

Make the red wine reduction. Bring the red wine to the boil in a wide-based saucepan, then simmer until it has reduced by three-quarters – you need exactly 50ml (2fl oz/scant ¼ cup), so measure to check and reduce further if needed. Add the mushroom stock and bay leaf and bring to the boil, simmer again until it has reduced by two-thirds in volume – you need exactly 350ml (12fl oz/1½ cups) of reduced stock, so measure to check, and reduce further if necessary.

FOR THE MUSHROOMS

200ml (7fl oz/generous ¾ cup) mushroom stock (see page 65)

4 king oyster mushrooms, base trimmed

250g (9oz) chestnut mushrooms, stalks removed

100g (3½oz) shimeji mushrooms, trimmed and base removed

2 tbsp extra virgin olive oil

sea salt, to sprinkle

FOR THE GARNISH

½ x quantity of cavolo nero crisps (see page 28)

KING OYSTER MUSHROOMS

King oyster mushrooms are large, meaty mushrooms that look a little like porcinis (or ceps) but have a meatier texture and more delicate flavour. They benefit from being a farmable mushroom and so are more readily available than porcinis. If you cannot find any then you can substitute porcinis, pied bleu or even quarters of peeled portobello mushrooms.

When ready to cook, put 4 litres (7 pints/16 cups) of cold water and 40g (1½oz/2½ tbsp) of salt in a large lidded saucepan and bring to the boil. Line a baking tray (sheet) with kitchen (paper) towel and have a clean tea towel to keep the cooked tortellini warm.

Cut each king oyster mushroom "log" into 7mm (⅓ inch) slices. Cut each chestnut mushroom in half across the middle to give 2 flat discs, then cut these into 7mm (⅓ inch) discs. Slice the shimeji mushrooms.

Heat 1 tablespoon of olive oil in a small frying pan (skillet) and add the king oyster mushroom slices. Sprinkle with a little salt, brown one side to a golden brown and then flip and colour the other side. Add the mushroom stock and reduce it down to make a glaze, then keep warm.

Heat the remaining olive oil in a frying pan (skillet) and add the chestnut mushrooms, sprinkle with a little salt and fry for 2 minutes. Add the shimeji mushrooms and continue to cook until the liquid has released from the mushrooms and evaporated again. Add 4 tablespoons of the red wine reduction and cook to thicken slightly, then keep warm until needed.

Now cook your pasta. Turn the temperature down so the water is at a gentle simmer. Gently place no more than 5 tortellini into the saucepan of simmering water and stir gently to prevent them from sticking to the base. You need to cook them for only 1–2 minutes – they will float to the surface and the pasta will be firm but cooked – it must have bite. As soon as they are done, carefully remove them, one at a time, using a slotted spoon and put on the lined baking tray (sheet). Cover with a tea towel to keep warm and prepare the next 5. Repeat until they are all cooked. Once they are all cooked place 3–5 tortellini into each of 4 pasta bowls. Spoon the diced mushrooms over the top of each and then arrange the king oyster mushroom slices on top.

Pour the mushroom reduction into the bottom of the bowl. Add a cavolo nero crisp to each bowl and serve immediately.

I love using what are normally perceived as the cheapest ingredients and giving them a luxury treatment. Really, there are no second-class plants: potatoes are equal to truffles, and I see no reason why you shouldn't take the same time and care with every ingredient, be it a potato or a truffle.

Serves: 4

POTATO LINGUINE
with an oyster mushroom and white wine sauce

FOR THE POTATO LINGUINE
1.2kg (2½lb) large baking potatoes (not peeled)
sea salt

FOR THE SAUCE
150g (5½oz/generous 1 cup) pine nuts
275ml (9½fl oz/1⅛ cups) water
35ml (1¼fl oz/7 tsp) black truffle oil
85ml (3fl oz/⅓ cup) extra virgin olive oil
3 banana shallots, finely diced
375ml (12½fl oz/generous 1½ cups) dry white wine
100g (3½oz) thin-leaved cabbage leaves
400g (14oz) oyster mushrooms, sliced to 5mm (¼-inch) strips
sea salt

FOR THE GARNISH
black pepper
1 small black truffle

Using a spiralizer, turn the potatoes into long, linguine-shaped strings. Separate the strands, removing any offcuts, and place in a large bowl. Weigh the potato and add 1.5 per cent of the weight in salt (for 500g (1lb 2oz) of potato add 7.5g (¼oz/1¼ tsp) of salt). Carefully mix the salt through the potatoes, taking care not to break the strands, and leave for 1 hour, then rinse in cold water and drain.

Meanwhile, make the oyster mushroom and white wine sauce. Put the pine nuts, water and truffle oil into a blender and blend until the mix is completely smooth and creamy with no lumps. Heat 35ml (1¼fl oz/7 tsp) of the olive oil in a large frying pan (skillet), add the shallots and fry until just soft but without colour. Add the wine and cook to reduce by three-quarters, then add the pine nut cream and heat until the sauce thickens. Season to taste with salt (see page 15) and set aside. Separate out the cabbage leaves and remove the thick stems. Stack 5 leaves on top of each other, roll into a cigar shape and finely shred. Set aside.

Gently heat the rest of the olive oil in a large saucepan. Add the oyster mushrooms and a pinch of salt and fry until just cooked. Add the white wine sauce and gently bring to the boil, then add the potato linguine and, if needed, a little water so the sauce covers the potato. Simmer gently, for up to 10 minutes, adding a little more water if necessary so the sauce always covers the linguine, until the potato is cooked. Don't add too much water, though, or your sauce will be too liquid. Once the potato is almost cooked add the cabbage, press it into the sauce and boil hard to thicken the sauce and cook the cabbage. Gently stir to combine, taking care not to break the linguine.

When cooked, remove from the heat and leave for 1 minute. Then, using a carving fork, twist about a quarter of the linguine into a roll and transfer to a plate. Repeat until you have 4 rolls on 4 plates and then spoon any remaining sauce over the top. Add a grind of black pepper, liberally grate black truffle over the top and serve.

ALTERNATIVES

If you don't want to make the potato linguine, or prefer to use real pasta, then simply buy the best-quality linguine you can find and cook it according to the method on page 127. Cook the sauce and stir in the cooked pasta at the last minute.

Italian food is all about simplicity. It is about using fantastic produce, treating it with respect and mastering the tiny details of apparently easy food. Gnocchi is the ultimate expression of this philosophy; it is so simple, yet so hard to do really well.

Almond milk contains starches from the almonds so will thicken naturally when heated. It also thickens further in the presence of an acid. Because of this there is no need to add starch or a roux to your almond sauces, they will thicken nicely all on their own.

Serves: 4

POTATO GNOCCHI
with summer peas and spinach in an almond white wine sauce

FOR THE POTATO GNOCCHI
800g (1lb 12oz) potatoes
(preferably russet or king Edward, baking potatoes as a fall back)
135g (4¾oz/1 cup) type 00
flour (may be more or less if calculating the ratio weight)

FOR THE SAUCE
1 x quantity of almond milk (see page 221)
200g (7oz/1⅓ cups) freshly podded peas
25ml (1fl oz/5 tsp) extra virgin olive oil
1 small onion, finely diced
125ml (4fl oz/½ cup) dry white wine
200ml (7fl oz/generous ¾ cup) basic stock (see page 64)
30ml (1fl oz/2 tbsp) lemon juice
3g (3½ tsp) chopped summer savory or tarragon leaves (optional)
sea salt
100g (3½oz/3⅓ cups) spinach

FOR THE GARNISH
1 lemon
black pepper
white truffle oil

Make the almond milk (see page 221) in advance as the almonds need to soak overnight.

Make the basic stock (see page 64) and the gnocchi (see page 138), weighing out the cooked potato and adding 30 per cent of the cooked weight in flour. Alternatively, use 400g (14oz) of cooked potatoes and 135g (4¾oz/1 cup) of flour.

Blanch the peas for 2–3 minutes then shock in ice-cold water (see page 185) and set aside.

Heat the olive oil in a large saucepan over a low heat. Add the onion and fry gently for about 2 minutes until translucent but not coloured. Add the white wine and simmer gently to reduce by two-thirds, then add the stock and continue to simmer until it has reduced by half. Add the almond milk and simmer gently to thicken. When it is just thick enough to coat the back of a metal spoon, remove from the heat and add the lemon juice and summer savory. Season with salt to taste.

When the sauce is nearly ready, cook the gnocchi (see page 138). Then add the gnocchi, peas and spinach to the sauce and gently warm through. If the sauce has become too thick, dilute with a little water until it is the desired consistency.

Spoon the gnocchi onto 4 plates. Zest a quarter of a lemon over each plate, add a few twists of black pepper and a very generous drizzle of white truffle oil. Serve immediately.

GNOCCHI TROUBLE-SHOOTING

- *If the gnocchi is tough and/or leathery – you kneaded the dough too much.*
- *If the gnocchi is hard – you added too much flour.*
- *If the gnocchi breaks up in the water – you didn't add enough flour.*
- *If the gnocchi cracks as you roll it – you didn't work fast enough and the dough cooled too much. You can knead it to return elasticity, but the end product will be tougher.*
- *If the gnocchi dough is wet and sticky and you've already added lots of flour – you either mashed your potato and made it gluey, chose a wet or buttery variety of potato, or didn't take enough care to get the moisture from the potato.*

| HOW TO MAKE POTATO GNOCCHI |

Most gnocchi recipes you come across outside of Italy contain egg, but within Italy there is a lively debate about whether it should or not. Gnocchi made using just flour and potato is the purest way of working. It creates a beautiful, light gnocchi where the flavour of the potato can really sing through. It also makes it hard to work with. The following will help point you in the right direction, until you develop a feel for it.

• Every potato has a different water content so you can never say for sure how much flour you will need. Add 30 per cent of the cooked potato weight, and then a little more if the mix is still too sticky.

• The variety of potato you buy matters more than anything else: russets and king Edwards are your best choices. Otherwise use baking potatoes as they are selected to be fluffy regardless of their variety.

• Always use a potato ricer to mash the potato. Using a masher will risk making the potato gluey before you've even started, and the potato needs to be light and fluffy.

• Work very fast – the mix is easy to work with while warm and becomes harder and harder as it cools.

• The first time you make gnocchi, it's unlikely to be perfect. Don't worry or give up at the first hurdle, be willing to give it five goes before you become despondent, or try making cavatelli instead (see page 122) to get a feel for it.

• You are not trying to knead the dough as you would knead bread, but merely incorporate the flour as you would for a shortbread. If you knead it, your gnocchi will be tough.

• Buying a ridged pasta board will make your life infinitely easier. You can roll gnocchi on a fork, but it's hard and you'll be there for the rest of your life!

Preheat the oven to (fan) 160°C/180°C/350°F/gas mark 4. Line a small baking tray (sheet) with 200g (7oz/¾ cup) of fine sea salt. Place the potatoes on the salt and cut 3 long slits in the top of each potato. Bake in the oven for 1 hour or until completely soft, then remove and discard the salt.

Holding the potatoes in a tea towel, cut them in half lengthways to allow the steam to escape and leave for 3-4 minutes. Scoop the flesh out and put it through a potato ricer, with the smallest disc inserted. Weigh the potatoes, then work out 30 per cent of that weight, and measure out that amount of flour (for example, for 500g (1lb 2oz) of potato, weigh 150g (5½oz) of flour.

Scatter the potato over a clean work surface and sieve half the flour over the top. With your fingertips, mix the flour in and then sprinkle the remaining flour over the top. Gently fold the mix over to incorporate the flour and press it down to form a smooth, light dough. If it feels very wet or sticky add a little more flour until workable. Knead twice.

Lightly flour your work surface, form the dough into a log and roll it in the flour. Working quickly to prevent the mix from cooling too fast, cut the dough into equal eighths and then roll each piece into a 1cm (½-inch) wide sausage. Cut each sausage into 1.5cm (½-inch) lengths. Keep the rest of the dough under a clean tea towel.

Using the fleshy part of your thumb, flatten each ball slightly against a gnocchi board, butter pat or large fork and then roll it downwards to form a gnocchi shape with a little crease in the bottom where it folded over. Press hard enough to create a ridge, but not so hard you flatten the gnocchi. Allow each gnocchi to roll onto the work surface. If they are a little sticky dust the surface very lightly in fine semolina. When you've made all the gnocchi, spread them out on a board lined with non-stick baking parchment.

Bring a large saucepan with 4 litres (7 pints/16 cups) of water and 40g (1½oz/2½ tbsp) of salt to the boil. When the water is boiling, carefully add the gnocchi in 2 batches. Try not to fiddle with it too much or you risk sticking them together. If you think they may stick to the bottom, stir the water on the surface to form a vortex without touching the gnocchi.

Once the gnocchi float to the surface, cook for a further 30 seconds, then scoop out with a slotted spoon.

Asparagus lends itself so well to Italian food that sometimes it's hard to think outside of the classic Italian ingredients of lemon, pasta, herbs and garlic. This dish came about from considering asparagus differently, as a fern shoot, just emerging from the earthy bed of the forest floor – woody, nutty and grassy. The gnocchi is a quiet nod to the Italian association it will always hold in my mind.

Serves: 4

HAZELNUT GNOCCHI
with asparagus and a hazelnut sauce

FOR THE GNOCCHI

100g (3½oz/¾ cup) blanched hazelnuts

800g (1lb 12oz) baking potatoes

135g (4¾oz/1 cup) type 00 flour (may be more or less if calculating the ratio weight)

pinch of cayenne pepper

FOR THE SAUCE

50g (1¾oz/⅓ cup) blanched hazelnuts

20ml (4 tsp) extra virgin olive oil

100g (3½oz) sliced shallots

50ml (2fl oz/scant ¼ cup) white wine

15ml (1 tbsp) hazelnut oil

150ml (5fl oz/⅔ cup) cold water

3g (½ tsp) sea salt

cayenne pepper

nutmeg

FOR THE CHERVIL AND ASPARAGUS

1 x quantity of chervil purée (see page 182)

24 asparagus spears, trimmed and peeled

FOR THE GARNISH

15 candied hazelnuts (see page 116), split in half

hazelnut oil, to drizzle

Preheat the oven to (fan) 160°C/180°C/350°F/gas mark 4. Spread the hazelnuts for the gnocchi and the sauce out on 2 separate baking trays (sheets) and roast for 7 minutes until golden. Transfer the nuts for the gnocchi to a blender and process until a flour consistency. Set aside the nuts for the sauce.

Make the chervil purée (see page 182) and candied hazelnuts (see page 116).

Bake and rice the baking potatoes following the method on page 138 for making gnocchi. Weigh the potatoes, then measure out 20 per cent of the weight in the blended hazelnuts and 30 per cent of the weight in flour (see page 138). Alternatively, measure out 400g (14oz) of cooked potatoes, 80g (2¾oz) of blended hazelnuts and 135g (4¾oz) of flour. Make the gnocchi following the method on page 138, then shock in ice-cold water (see page 185), drain and set aside.

Heat the olive oil in a small saucepan and fry the shallots until soft but not coloured. Add the wine and cook until it has evaporated. Put the roasted hazelnuts into a blender with the cooked shallots, hazelnut oil, measured water and salt and process until silky smooth (adding a little water if needed to create a pourable, smooth consistency). Add a tiny pinch of cayenne pepper and a few twists of nutmeg, then pass through a fine sieve into a bowl.

Bring a large saucepan of water to the boil and add a large handful of salt. When boiling, add the asparagus and cook for about 2 minutes until tender, then remove immediately using a slotted spoon and put into a large bowl.

Put the hazelnut gnocchi and hazelnut sauce in a small saucepan and heat gently, adding a little water if necessary to prevent it from becoming too thick and splitting.

Spread 2 tablespoons of chervil purée around the outside of each of 4 large plates. Pile the asparagus in the centre with the gnocchi and sauce next to it. Scatter a few candied hazelnuts over the top, drizzle a little hazelnut oil around the plate and serve.

In the codified world of Italian cookery this wouldn't classify as a risotto, lacking butter and Parmesan cheese, and it certainly wouldn't classify as a risotto Milanese, lacking the addition of bone marrow. However, the idea of a rich, unctuous rice dish flavoured with saffron is a good one and entirely in keeping with food made from plants. Italians would call this a saffron rice, which lacks the romance of the original title, so in recognition of the fact that recipes evolve constantly and if we fix a recipe we kill it, I am going to stick with the original title.

Serves: 4

RISOTTO MILANESE
with peas and pine nuts

2 litres (3½ pints/8 cups) mushroom & fennel stock (see page 65)

50–100g (1¾oz–3½oz) freshly podded peas

3g (½ tsp) sea salt

1g (½ tbsp) saffron

50ml (2fl oz/scant ¼ cup) extra virgin olive oil

2 banana shallots, finely diced

4 cloves of garlic, puréed (see page 147)

400g (14oz/generous 2 cups) carnaroli rice

250ml (8½fl oz/1 cup) white wine

125g (4½oz) pine nut butter (see page 221)

25ml (1fl oz/5 tsp) white truffle oil, plus extra to drizzle

20g (¾oz/2½ tbsp) pine nuts

black pepper

Make the mushroom & fennel stock (see page 65).

Put the peas in a small saucepan, add 200ml (7fl oz/generous ¾ cup) of stock and the salt. Bring to the boil, simmer for 2–4 minutes until the peas are cooked, then remove them with a slotted spoon and leave to cool. When cool, pop the peas out of their skins and set aside. Leave the stock in the saucepan.

Grind the saffron to a powder using a pestle and mortar. Add 50ml (2fl oz/ scant ¼ cup) of hot stock, mix well, then set aside.

Heat the olive oil in a saucepan, add the shallot and fry gently until translucent. Add the garlic and fry until cooked, then stir in the rice. Add the wine and cook until completely evaporated. Add 4 ladles of hot stock and cook, stirring constantly, until it has almost disappeared. Add another ladle of stock and continue to stir until it has almost disappeared. Keep adding stock, 1 ladle at a time, until the rice is three-quarters cooked and is thick and stiff – it should be soft but with a chalky texture on the tongue.

Add the saffron stock and keep stirring. Once cooked, remove from the heat and add the pine nut butter and truffle oil. Stir once and allow it to melt into the mix, then vigorously mix it to emulsify the rice. It should be glossy and unctuous, with a just pourable consistency – add a little more stock if needed.

Season the risotto to taste with salt (see page 15) and divide it between the bowls. Scatter over the peas and pine nuts, add a twist of black pepper and a drizzle of white truffle oil, then serve.

This dish heralds the coming of the colder months. The hearty texture of the barley, the bitter radicchio, the hint of smoke from the hazelnuts, a twist of nutmeg, it all comes together into something that is gently seductive, the culinary equivalent of blankets and wine in front of a fire with loved ones.

Serves: 4

PARSNIP BARLEY RISOTTO
with poached pears and smoked hazelnuts

FOR THE POACHED PEARS

2 Williams pears
250ml (8½fl oz/1 cup) basic stock (see page 64)
250ml (8½fl oz/1 cup) white wine
2 sprigs of thyme
5g (⅛oz/1 tsp) sea salt
50g (1¾oz/¼ cup) caster (superfine) sugar
hazelnut oil, to fry

FOR THE RISOTTO

1 x quantity of parsnip & shallot purée (see page 184)
40ml (1½fl oz/8 tsp) extra virgin olive oil
40g (1½oz) diced banana shallots
3 cloves of garlic, puréed (see page 147)
200g (7oz/1 cup) pearl barley
225ml (7½fl oz/scant 1 cup) white wine
1.5 litres (2½ pints/6 cups) basic stock (see page 64)
sea salt

FOR THE ROAST PARSNIPS

2 large parsnips, peeled and trimmed
2 sprigs of thyme
1 bay leaf
2 pieces of mace
25ml (1fl oz/5 tsp) extra virgin olive oil
good pinch of sea salt

Prepare the basic stock (see page 64), parsnip & shallot purée (see page 184), smoked hazelnuts (see page 116) and pickled pear (see page 100).

Make the poached pears. Peel each pear, cut in half lengthways, then remove the core and stalk. Place the pear halves in a saucepan with the rest of the poaching ingredients (but not the hazelnut oil) and gently bring to the boil. Simmer gently for 5–10 minutes. As soon as the pears are softening – a knife should easily pass through the thickest part – remove from the heat and leave to cool in the saucepan.

Make the barley risotto base. Heat the olive oil in a saucepan, then add the shallot and fry gently until soft. Add the puréed garlic and cook for 2 minutes, then add the pearl barley and stir. Add the wine and cook until it has all evaporated, then add 500ml (18fl oz/2 cups) of stock and bring to the boil. Simmer gently until the stock has almost disappeared, stirring often and vigorously. Add another 250ml (8½fl oz/1 cup) of stock and cook until this has disappeared. Keep adding the stock in batches and cook until the barley is soft but still has a "pop", and the stock has all evaporated. Note you may not need to use all the stock. When ready, transfer to a large baking tray (sheet) and spread out evenly to cool quickly.

Preheat the oven to (fan) 160°C/180°C/350°F/gas mark 4. Put a 45cm (18-inch) strip of baking parchment on a baking tray (sheet). Cut the parsnips into quarters lengthways, then chop to 1cm (½-inch) dice. Mix the parsnip, thyme, bay leaf, mace, olive oil and salt in a large bowl, then transfer the mix to the centre of the paper, fold in half, and roll up the edges to form a sealed parcel. Bake in the oven for 20 minutes until just soft. Remove the parsnip and set aside.

Put the radicchio leaves in a bowl, add a generous glug of hazelnut oil and a pinch of salt and toss well using your fingers.

Halve each smoked hazelnut and place in a small bowl with a little hazelnut oil and a small pinch of salt.

Put the barley risotto into a saucepan and add the parsnip & shallot purée. If very thick, add a little water. Warm gently, stirring. Once hot, check the consistency – it should be pourable but appear thick and creamy. Taste and season with salt (see page 15), then keep warm.

FOR THE RADICCHIO
12 red radicchio leaves
hazelnut oil
sea salt

FOR THE GARNISH
20g (¾oz/2½ tbsp) smoked
    hazelnuts, halved (see page 116),
1 x quantity of pickled pear (see
    page 100)
hazelnut oil
pinch of sea salt
1 nutmeg clove

While you warm the risotto, remove the poached pears from their liquid and pat dry with kitchen (paper) towel. Line a frying pan (skillet) with a sheet of non-stick baking parchment and get it very hot. Add a splash of hazelnut oil and place the pears, cut side down, on the paper. Press down and cook at a high temperature until the surface is very dark, almost burnt. Remove from the pan and cut a slice from the back of each pear so it will sit up at an angle. Place just off centre on each of 4 large plates.

Check the risotto consistency, adding a little more water if too thick. Fold half the diced parsnip mix into the risotto. Spoon 1 tablespoon of risotto mix next to each pear. Lay a radicchio leaf on top, then add another 4 tablespoons of risotto on top of the leaf. Add another radicchio leaf and another 4 tablespoons of risotto then top with a radicchio leaf. Scatter the hazelnuts over the plate, then scatter the remaining diced parsnip over the top. Place 7 pieces of pickled pear across each plate and drizzle over hazelnut oil. Finely grate a little nutmeg over the top and serve.

PURÉEING GARLIC

I don't recommend using garlic crushers/presses, so this is my tried and tested way of puréeing garlic. Using a large knife, cut the woody root end from the clove. Place the flat side of the knife's blade against the garlic and crush the clove until you hear a crunch. The clove should now come cleanly away from the skin. Discard the skin and on a chopping board slice the garlic as thinly as you can, then chop it as finely as you can. Bring it into a small pile and sprinkle with a large pinch of salt. With the flat of the blade, crush the pile of garlic and draw it towards you, smearing it against the board. Collect it all back up into a pile and crush and smear it again. Continue doing this until you have a smooth purée.

A good mushroom risotto should have a lot of mushrooms and a lot of umami (see page 16) – this version has both.

The trick to really well-cooked mushrooms is to use a large pan and a high heat so they don't stew in their own juices. Try to cook the mushrooms alongside the risotto mix so you can combine them when the rice is ready.

Serves: 4

PERFECT MUSHROOM RISOTTO

FOR THE DOUBLE MUSHROOM STOCK

1.5 litres (2½ pints/6¼ cups) mushroom stock (see page 65)

50g (1¾oz) dried shiitake or porcini mushrooms

FOR THE MUSHROOM PURÉE

40ml (1½fl oz/8 tsp) extra virgin olive oil

190g (6¾oz) chestnut mushrooms, sliced

115ml (4fl oz/½ cup) ruby port

30g (1¼oz) dried mushrooms (reserved from the double mushroom stock)

12ml (2½ tsp) red wine vinegar

15ml (1 tbsp) truffle oil

45ml (1½fl oz/3 tbsp) double mushroom stock (reserved from above)

FOR THE RISOTTO

2 king oyster mushrooms

200g (7oz) chestnut mushrooms

2 large portobello mushrooms

1 head shimeji mushrooms

75ml (2¾fl oz/⅓ cup) extra virgin olive oil

sea salt

100g (3½oz/½ cup) diced banana shallots

4 cloves of garlic, puréed (see page 147)

350g (12oz/1¾ cups) carnaroli rice

double mushroom stock (see above)

First make the mushroom stock (see page 65), then the double mushroom stock. In a saucepan bring the mushroom stock to the boil, then remove from the heat. Add the dried mushrooms, cover with a lid and leave for 30 minutes. Drain the stock into a separate saucepan and set aside. Reserve the dried mushrooms for the mushroom purée.

Make the mushroom purée. Heat the olive oil in a wide-based saucepan. Add the chestnut mushrooms and sweat until the juices have evaporated. Add the ruby port and reduce until a thick syrup. Remove from the heat and transfer to a blender. Add the rest of the ingredients to the blender and blend until silky smooth, adding a little water only if necessary.

Prepare and cook the mushrooms for the risotto. Cut the king oyster mushrooms into 5mm (¼-inch) slices. Quarter the chestnut mushrooms, slice the portobello mushrooms and trim the woody base from the shimeji mushrooms. To cook the fried mushrooms, heat 50ml (2fl oz/scant ¼ cup) of olive oil in a large, deep frying pan (skillet). Add the oyster mushrooms and cook for 2 minutes. Add the chestnut mushrooms and a small pinch of salt and cook for 1 minute. Add the portobello mushrooms with another small pinch of salt and cook for about 4 minutes until all the mushrooms are three-quarters cooked. Add the shimeji mushrooms and cook until all the mushrooms are cooked through (but not withered) and all the liquid is gone. Adjust the seasoning (see page 15).

Once the mushrooms are on the go, cook the rest of the risotto. Heat the double mushroom stock in a saucepan and bring to a gentle simmer. Heat the remaining olive oil in a frying pan (skillet), add the shallot and fry gently until translucent. Add the garlic and fry until cooked, then add the rice and stir well. Add 4 ladles of hot stock and cook, stirring constantly, until it has almost disappeared. Add another ladle of stock and continue to stir until it has almost disappeared. Keep adding stock, 1 ladle at a time, until the rice is nearly but not quite cooked through, about 15–20 minutes. You may not need all the stock, or you may need to add a little extra hot water. The texture will be thick, creamy and stiff.

When the risotto is cooked, add the fried mushrooms and remove from the heat. Add the mushroom purée and stir well to combine. Taste and adjust the seasoning (see page 15), divide between 4 bowls and serve.

Broccoli has a majestic shape and a deep, satisfying flavour when cooked well. The standard way of preparing broccoli by cutting off the florets and discarding the stem is such a waste as the stem is just as edible as the flower heads. Preparing it this way, which has become my go-to technique, not only shows off its dramatic shape but also delivers a broad surface area for the Maillard reaction to take place (see page 177), resulting in a striking, delicious plate of food. Just remember to allow time to soak the spelt and lettuce.

Serves: 4

SEARED CALABRESE BROCCOLI
with spelt grain, a smoked almond emulsion and candied almonds

FOR THE SPELT GRAIN
300g (10½oz/1¾ cups) pearled
    spelt grain
500ml (18fl oz/2 cups) water
5g (⅛oz/1 tsp) sea salt

FOR THE COS LETTUCE
1.25g (¼ tsp) sea salt
250ml (8½fl oz/1 cup) cold water
1 cos lettuce head

FOR THE BROCCOLI
1 large broccoli head
oil, for frying
sea salt

FOR THE SMOKED ALMOND EMULSION
25g (1oz/2¾ tbsp) smoked almonds
    (see page 116)
25g (1oz/3 tbsp) smoked cashew
    nuts (see page 116)
90ml (3¼fl oz/generous ⅓ cup)
    high-quality olive oil
100ml (3½fl oz/scant ½ cup) water
1.5g (¼ tsp) sea salt
pinch of cayenne pepper

FOR THE GARNISH
4 tbsp drained pickled cabbage
    (see page 100) or sauerkraut
    (see page 101)
candied almonds (see page 116)
12 lovage leaves, coarsely shredded

Put the spelt into a bowl, cover with cold water and leave to soak for at least 4 hours – and ideally overnight – in the fridge.

Mix the salt and water together for the cos lettuce and leave so the salt dissolves completely into the water to make a saline solution. Remove and discard the outer 3 or 4 leaves from the lettuce. Cut the lettuce into quarters lengthways and submerge in the saline solution. Place in the fridge for at least 4 hours – or ideally overnight.

Prepare the pickled cabbage (see page 100), candied almonds (see page 116), smoked almonds (see page 116) and smoked cashew nuts (see page 116).

Drain and rinse the spelt, then put into a small saucepan with the measured water and salt. Cover with a lid, bring to the boil, then simmer gently for about 10 minutes until the spelt is soft but still pops in the mouth. Drain and rinse in cold water.

Meanwhile, peel the stalk of the broccoli, removing any woody parts. Cut the broccoli in half through the centre of the stalk. Cut each half in half again through the centre of the stalk and then again to give 8 wedges. Using a peeler, neaten up each wedge.

Put all the smoked almond emulsion ingredients together in a blender and process until silky smooth and glossy.

Take the cos lettuce out of the saline solution. Select 8 lettuce leaves and cut them in half, forming sharp wedges. Form the pickled cabbage into 4 neat balls.

Heat a little oil in a large frying pan (skillet). Fry the broccoli wedges on each side, seasoning well with salt, until dark and crispy. Cover with a lid and remove from the heat. Set aside for 4 minutes to soften in their own steam.

Put the spelt and smoked almond emulsion into a small saucepan and heat gently until hot, but do not boil. Check and adjust the seasoning and keep warm.

Put 6 tablespoons of spelt mix in each of 4 large pasta bowls. Place 1 or 2 wedges of cooked broccoli upright on top of the spelt and add a ball of pickled cabbage. Add 2 shards of lettuce and then scatter with candied almonds and shredded lovage leaves. Serve hot.

Before I made the decision to go completely plant-based this was one of my favourite snacks, reminiscent of lazy mornings in Spain drinking strong bitter coffee and looking out across the mountains. I decided to create my own version of tortilla after being served so many sad, limp imitations in vegan cafés along with that other poorly made vegan classic, the farinita. This dish is a hybrid: it takes the technique from a tortilla de patatas and the flavour and depth from a well-made farinita. Dare I say it, I think I prefer this to the classic, egg-bound version, and it certainly keeps better for the next day. Just make sure you prepare the gram flour batter a day or two ahead.

Serves: 4–8

TORTILLA DE PATATAS
with crushed tomato salad

FOR THE TORTILLA
100g (3½oz/scant 1 cup) gram flour
150ml (5fl oz/⅔ cup) water
800g (1lb 12oz) floury potatoes
    (baking, maris piper or rooster
    work well)
500–750ml (18–26ml/2–3 cups)
    olive oil
1 brown onion, sliced
5g (⅛oz/1 tsp) sea salt

FOR THE SALAD
4 large, ripe, sweet tomatoes (the
    best you can buy)
15ml (1 tbsp) olive oil
5ml (1 tsp) sherry vinegar
1g (scant ¼ tsp) sea salt
1 small shallot (not a banana
    shallot), finely diced
10 tarragon leaves, diced

TO SERVE
everyday bread (see page 212)

Sieve the gram flour into a small sterile jug (see page 101) and whisk in the water to form a smooth batter. Put somewhere warm (22°C/71°F) for 24–48 hours. The longer the fermentation time, the better the flavour.

When ready to cook, prepare the tomato salad. Blanch, shock and peel the tomatoes (see page 84), then cut into 5mm (¼-inch) dice. Put in a small bowl with the oil, sherry vinegar and salt. Crush gently with a fork, then add the shallot and tarragon. Stir everything together and set aside for the flavours to mingle.

Cut the unpeeled potatoes into 1cm (½-inch) dice and place in a saucepan. Completely cover with the olive oil. Gently heat the oil until it starts to boil, stirring gently to prevent the potatoes from sticking. Once the oil is bubbling, add the onion and simmer, gently stirring often, for 10–15 minutes until the potato is cooked. Once cooked, immediately pour the mix through a sieve set over a saucepan, allowing all the oil to drip through. While the potato is piping hot, tip into a large bowl, stir in the salt and add the gram flour batter. Stir to mix well.

Put a couple of tablespoons of the oil into a non-stick 23cm (9-inch) frying pan (skillet) and heat gently. When hot, tip the potato mix into the pan, flatten it down and press to make sure there are no gaps. Fry gently until firm and the bottom is golden brown.

Make sure the tortilla is loose in the pan, then firmly holding a plate over the top, turn the pan over to deposit the tortilla on the plate. Slide the tortilla back into the frying pan (skillet) and fry until the underside is golden brown. Turn out onto a board and allow to cool to room temperature before cutting into slices and serving with the crushed tomato salad and bread.

Croquetas are a traditional Spanish tapas made from a thick white sauce, usually with added ham, which are breaded and deep fried so the outside is crisp and the inside is melting and delicious. This dish makes use of the magical qualities of cashew nuts to create a similar effect, but with only the one ingredient. Cashews contain a lot of natural starches and fats and so, once puréed, they can fulfil the role of the roux, milk and cheese in the recipe all on their own. The full culinary potential of cashews is only just being realized – heat them up and wonderful things begin to happen.

Serves: 4

SMOKED CASHEW CROQUETAS
with port-glazed red beetroot (beets) and orange emulsion

FOR THE CROQUETAS
300g (10½oz/2⅓ cups) smoked cashew nuts (see page 116)
750ml (26fl oz/3 cups) water
10g (¼oz/1¾ tsp) sea salt
cayenne pepper
200g (7oz/1⅔ cups) plain (all-purpose) flour
400g (14oz/3⅔ cups) panko breadcrumbs
sunflower oil, for deep-fat frying

FOR THE GLAZED BEETROOT (BEETS)
6 round red beetroot (beets)
550ml (19fl oz/2¼ cups) water
1 onion, finely sliced
2 sticks of celery, sliced
1 bay leaf
20 black peppercorns
100ml (3½fl oz/scant ½ cup) red wine
125ml (4fl oz/½ cup) ruby port

FOR THE ORANGE EMULSION
2 oranges
15g (½oz/1 tbsp) Dijon mustard
5g (⅛oz/1 tsp) caster (superfine) sugar
100ml (3½fl oz/scant ½ cup) rapeseed oil

Prepare the smoked cashew nuts (see page 116), then add to a blender with 500ml (18fl oz/2 cups) of the water and the salt. Blend until very smooth. Transfer to a small saucepan and heat gently, stirring all the time – as it comes to the boil it will thicken dramatically. Check the seasoning and adjust if necessary (see page 15). Add a small pinch of cayenne pepper and transfer to a small bowl. Cover with cling film (plastic wrap) in contact with the surface of the mix and place in the fridge to chill.

Preheat the oven to (fan) 160°C/180°C/350°F/gas mark 4. Make the mixed toasted seeds (see page 114).

Take a large piece of foil and wrap the beetroot (beets) and 50ml (2fl oz/scant ¼ cup) of the water tightly in it, making a watertight parcel. Put on a baking tray (sheet) and bake in the oven for 1 hour until soft, then leave to cool in the foil. Once cold, remove from the foil and transfer any liquid into a saucepan. Rub the skin from the beetroot (beets) and put the skin into the saucepan.

Line a chopping board with 4 sheets of cling film (plastic wrap) to stop staining, and use plastic gloves. Cut the top and bottom from each beetroot (beet), then cut each one into 1cm (½-inch) thick slices. You need 20 slices. Using a vegetable peeler, trim the edges from each disc to round it off neatly. Set aside.

Add the beetroot (beet) offcuts to the saucepan with the skin, along with the onion, celery, bay leaf, peppercorns and the rest of the measured water (500ml/17fl oz/ 2 cups). Bring to the boil and simmer for 20 minutes. Remove from the heat, allow to cool completely, then strain and return 200ml (7fl oz/generous ¾ cup) of the beetroot (beet) stock to a clean saucepan. Boil the stock rapidly to reduce until it begins to thicken noticeably, almost completely evaporating. Add the red wine and port and simmer to reduce by three-quarters.

Meanwhile, make the orange emulsion. Finely grate the zest from the oranges and then juice the oranges. Check you have 200ml (7fl oz/generous ¾ cup), and add a little more if necessary. Put the zest and juice into a small saucepan and simmer gently until reduced by half. Remove from the heat and allow to cool completely, then add the mustard and sugar and mix to combine.

FOR THE GARNISH

mixed toasted seeds (see page 114)
handful of watercress
handful of red mustard frill
extra virgin olive oil

Using a stick blender to emulsify, slowly add the rapeseed oil and blend until it is thick and glossy. This will keep for up to 3 days in the fridge.

Finish the croquetas. Put half the flour onto a plate and the other half into a large bowl. Whisk the remaining measured water (250ml/8fl oz/1 cup) into the bowl to form a thin batter. Place the breadcrumbs on a plate. Transfer the croquetas mix to a piping bag fitted with a 2cm (¾-inch) round nozzle (tip). Prepare your deep-fat fryer (see page 26). Put the watercress and red mustard frill in a small bowl and dress with a little olive oil.

Pipe the croqueta mix in 5–6cm (2–2¼-inch) lengths onto the floured plate and carefully roll to coat them in the flour. Repeat until you have 8 perfect croquetas. With a knife, transfer them one at a time into the flour and water mix first and then into the breadcrumbs. Roll each one in the breadcrumbs, ensuring they are completely covered and then gently re-roll so you have a neat tube shape. Continue until all the mix is used.

Deep-fry the croquetas, in batches if necessary, until crispy and golden brown, then drain on kitchen (paper) towel. At the same time, put the beetroot (beet) discs into a large frying pan (skillet) and add the port glaze. Bring the glaze to a rapid boil and reduce it down until it forms a sticky shiny glaze. Turn the beetroot (beets) over in the glaze to make sure they are well covered – if the glaze is too thick, add a tiny splash of water.

Place 3 or 4 beetroot (beets) slices and 2 croquetas on each of 4 large plates. Drizzle the orange emulsion around the plate (remember it is a strong flavour). Scatter the dressed watercress and red mustard frill over each plate and then sprinkle with the toasted seeds. Serve hot.

There is no clearer expression of the flavour of potato than the baked potato. The crispy skin carries so much of the flavour and all of the nutrient load of the root. This recipe refines the texture of the basic baked potato and then plays with temperature contrasts and classic flavour combinations to produce an interesting, unusual dish with clear flavours and unexpected contrasts.

Serves: 4

BAKED POTATO CROQUETAS
with burnt apple sorbet, cider-braised leeks and hazelnut butter

FOR THE SORBET
800g (1lb 12oz) Bramley apples
40g (1½oz/¼ cup) brown sugar
75g (2¾oz/⅓ cup) caster (superfine) sugar
25ml (1fl oz/5 tsp) glucose syrup
100ml (3½fl oz/scant ½ cup) water
30ml (2 tbsp) single malt whisky
1g (⅓ tsp) xanthan gum
1g (scant ¼ tsp) sea salt

FOR THE CROQUETAS FILLING
500g (1lb 2oz) large baking potatoes (to give 250g (9oz) cooked potato)
20g (¾oz/4 tsp) Dijon mustard
500ml (18fl oz/2 cups) water
6g (⅛oz/1 tsp) sea salt
cayenne pepper
grated nutmeg
60ml (2¼fl oz/¼ cup) extra virgin olive oil
85g (3oz/⅔ cup) plain (all-purpose) flour

FOR THE CROQUETAS COATING
250ml (8½fl oz/1 cup) water
200g (7oz/1⅔ cups) plain (all-purpose) flour
400g (14oz/3⅔ cups) panko breadcrumbs
sunflower oil, for deep-fat frying

Prepare the hazelnut butter (see page 221) and garlic parsley oil (see page 220). Make the sorbet and croquetas filling at least 4 hours before needed so they can set.

Preheat the oven to (fan) 160°C/180°C/350°F/gas mark 4. Place the hazelnuts on a small baking tray (sheet) and roast in the oven for 7 minutes until golden. Set aside.

Quarter the apples for the sorbet and remove the core and stem. Cut into 2cm (¾-inch) chunks, then mix with the brown sugar in a bowl. Pour onto a baking tray (sheet) lined with baking parchment and bake for 60–90 minutes until well cooked and just browning around the edges. Weigh out 500g (1lb 2oz) of the roasted apples and place in a blender.

At the same time, cook the baked potatoes. Prick all over with a fork and bake for 60–90 minutes. You want a well-done potato with a lightly crispy skin. Once cooked, remove from the oven and put in a bowl. Cover the bowl with cling film (plastic wrap) and leave for 10 minutes to sweat (this should soften the skin).

Put the caster (superfine) sugar, glucose syrup and water for the sorbet into a small saucepan and heat gently until the sugar has dissolved. Check you have 100ml (3½fl oz/scant ½ cup) and add a little water if necessary. Add the whisky, xanthan and salt to the mix and blend until very smooth. Pass through a sieve into a lidded container and put in the fridge until cold. When cold, churn the sorbet in an ice-cream maker following the manufacturer's instructions, then transfer to the freezer.

Cut the baked potato into chunks and weigh 250g (9oz) of it into a blender. Add the mustard, water and salt and blend until very smooth. Pass the potato stock through a sieve into a bowl and stir in a little cayenne pepper and nutmeg.

Mix the olive oil and flour together in a saucepan. Heat gently until it begins to bubble. Cook for 20 seconds and then slowly pour in the potato stock, whisking all the time. Keep adding the potato stock until all used, whisking to ensure there are no lumps. Then stir continuously with a silicon spatula until the mix is boiling and very thick. Pour the mix into a container and cover with cling film (plastic wrap), in contact with the mix to prevent a skin forming, then put into the fridge until completely cold and thick.

FOR THE LEEKS

1 tbsp garlic parsley oil (see page 220)

2 large leeks, roots and green tops discarded

½ Savoy cabbage

25ml (1fl oz/5 tsp) extra virgin olive oil

sea salt

100ml (3½fl oz/scant ½ cup) dry cider

100ml (3½fl oz/scant ½ cup) water

FOR THE HAZELNUTS

hazelnut butter (see page 221)

20g (¾oz/2½ tbsp) hazelnuts

hazelnut oil

About 10 minutes before frying the croquetas, cut the leeks in half lengthways and rinse well, then finely slice. Separate out the cabbage leaves and wash, then shake dry. Lay 2 or 3 on top of each other, roll up into a cigar shape and finely slice. Repeat with the rest. Heat the olive oil in a large saucepan and add the leeks and a pinch of salt. Cook for 1 minute then add the garlic parsley oil. Continue to cook gently until just soft, then add the cider and water and simmer until reduced by half. Add the cabbage and another pinch of salt and cook until the cider is virtually gone and the cabbage is soft. Keep warm until needed.

Finish the croquetas. Put half the flour onto a plate and the other half into a large bowl. Whisk the measured water into the bowl to form a thin batter. Place the breadcrumbs on a large plate. Transfer the croquetas mix to a piping bag fitted with a 2cm (¾-inch) round nozzle (tip). Prepare your deep-fat fryer (see page 26).

Pipe the croquetas mix in 5–6cm (2–2¼-inch) lengths onto the floured plate and carefully roll to coat them in the flour. Repeat until you have 8 perfect croquetas. With a knife, transfer them one at a time into the flour and water mix first and then into the breadcrumbs. Roll each one in the breadcrumbs, ensuring they are completely covered and then gently re-roll so you have a neat tube shape. Continue until all the mix is used.

Deep-fry the croquetas, in batches if necessary, until crispy and golden brown, then drain on kitchen (paper) towel.

Pile the braised leek mix onto each plate and add 2 croquetas. Pipe dollops of hazelnut butter around each plate. Crush half the roasted hazelnuts and scatter in a pile among the croquetas. Place a scoop of sorbet on top. Halve the remaining hazelnuts and add on top of the hazelnut butter. dollops Finally, drizzle a little hazelnut oil over everything.

This nut roast is very special – it really tastes of nuts, and the gravy is made using long, slow cooking methods to achieve a beautiful depth and complexity of flavour. It is a lot of work to make all the elements, but they can each be made up to three days ahead and reheated when needed. Or you can make just the nut roast and gravy and add accompaniments of your choice.

Serves: 4

HAZELNUT ROAST
with cider apples, braised celeriac (celery root), potato galette and cider gravy

FOR THE NUT ROAST
1 large celeriac (celery root) (at least 900g/2lb to give 500g (1lb 2oz) peeled)
1 large onion
2 cloves of garlic, peeled but whole
25ml (1fl oz/5 tsp) rapeseed oil
8g (¼oz/1½ tsp) sea salt
100g (3½oz/¾ cup) hazelnuts
100g (3½oz/¾ cup) cashew nuts
50g (1¾oz/⅓ cup) sunflower seeds
30g (1¼oz/¼ cup) cornflour (cornstarch)
15g (½oz/1 tbsp) mustard (see page 41), or shop-bought wholegrain mustard
⅛ nutmeg, grated
rapeseed oil

FOR THE POTATO GALETTE
4 baking potatoes
1 onion, peeled
8g (¼oz/1½ tsp) sea salt
150ml (5fl oz/⅔ cup) water
rapeseed oil

FOR THE CIDER GRAVY
25ml (1fl oz/5 tsp) rapeseed oil
1 onion, sliced
1 leek, sliced
250g (9oz) button mushrooms, sliced
1 turnip, peeled and sliced
4 cloves of garlic, skin on, smashed
0.5g (¼ tsp) caraway seeds
15g (½oz/1¼ tbsp) caster (superfine) sugar
15ml (1 tbsp) cider vinegar

Preheat the oven to (fan) 160°C/180°C/350°F/gas mark 4. Prepare the garlic parsley oil (see page 220).

Prepare the nut roast. Peel the celeriac (celery root) and onion and cut into 2cm (¾-inch) chunks. Place in a large bowl along with the garlic, rapeseed oil and 3g (½ tsp) of the salt. Mix everything together, then spread out on a large baking tray (sheet). Cover the tray with tin foil and roast the celeriac (celery root) in the oven for 30–40 minutes until soft.

Meanwhile, put the hazelnuts and cashews on a baking tray (sheet) and roast for 7 minutes or until golden. Put the sunflower seeds in a frying pan (skillet) with a splash of oil and fry until dark golden. Transfer the seeds to a food processor, process until fine crumbs, then put in a large bowl. Put the cashews and hazelnuts in the food processor and pulse to a coarse crumb, with some lumps, then add to the sunflower seeds. Put the onions, garlic and celeriac into the food processor and pulse to a coarse mash. Add to the nuts and seeds and mix everything together. Add the cornflour (cornstarch), mustard, remaining 5g (1 tsp) of salt and grated nutmeg and mix well.

Lay out a 45cm (18-inch) strip of cling film (plastic wrap), then lay another strip on top. Spoon a quarter of the mix onto this and form into a rough sausage shape about 4cm (1½ inches) thick. Fold over the bottom edge of the cling film (plastic wrap) and roll the mix up to form a sausage about 3cm (1¼ inches) thick. Fold the cling film (plastic wrap) over and roll the sausage tightly in the cling film (plastic wrap). Twist one end of the cling film (plastic wrap) to tie it closed. Squeeze the air out of the other side and twist the other end to form a tight, round, water-tight sausage shape with no air pockets. Tie closed. Repeat with the remaining mix to make 4 sausages in total.

Bring a large saucepan of water to the boil and add the sausages. Turn down to a simmer and cook for 20 minutes, then remove one at a time and plunge into a bowl of ice-cold water. Once cool, transfer to the fridge for at least an hour but ideally overnight, to firm up.

Make the galette. Slice the potatoes and onion very finely on a mandolin, then transfer to a bowl with the salt. Mix well and leave for 30 minutes until soft and pliable.

Line a 900g (2lb) rectangular loaf tin (pan) with baking parchment and layer the potatoes right up to the top. Season well. Add the measured water and cover tightly with foil. Bake for 45 minutes or until a knife passes cleanly through the centre.

250ml (8½fl oz/1 cup) cider
20g (¾oz/4 tsp) tomato purée
2.5g (½ tsp) yeast extract (such as marmite), or 5ml (1 tsp) soy sauce)
750ml (26fl oz/3 cups) water, plus extra for flour paste
1 bay leaf
20g (¾oz) dried mushrooms
3g (½ tsp) sea salt
cornflour (cornstarch)

FOR THE CELERIAC (CELERY ROOT)

1 large celeriac (celery root) (at least 1kg/2¼lb) or several smaller ones, skin and roots removed
100ml (3½fl oz/scant ½ cup) cider gravy (see above)
100ml (3½fl oz/scant ½ cup) water
3g (½ tsp) sea salt

FOR THE CIDER-POACHED APPLES

150g (5½oz/¾ cup) caster (superfine) sugar
150ml (5fl oz/⅔ cup) water
250ml (8½fl oz/1 cup) dry cider
3g (½ tsp) sea salt
3 Granny Smith apples (or other tart variety), peeled

FOR THE BRUSSELS SPROUTS

1 tbsp rapeseed oil
20 Brussels sprouts, trimmed, cut in half and outer leaves discarded
sea salt
2 tbsp garlic parsley oil (see page 220)

Remove from the oven and carefully press down on the foil to compress it. Set aside to cool, then place in the fridge for 2 hours.

Make the cider gravy. Heat the rapeseed oil in a large saucepan until very hot, then add all the sliced vegetables, the garlic and the caraway seeds. Stir well and fry, stirring occasionally, on a high heat for up to 20 minutes until it begins to take a dark colour. While this is cooking, put the sugar in a heavy-bottomed saucepan and heat gently until it melts and forms a golden caramel. Add the vinegar and cook until it evaporates by half, then add the cider and stir.

Add the tomato purée and yeast extract to the saucepan with the vegetables. Stir well and then cook for 5–10 minutes until a crust begins to form on the bottom of the saucepan (do not let this burn). Deglaze the saucepan by adding the sugar and cider mix and stir until the crust has dissolved, then bring to the boil and simmer until the cider has reduced by half. Add the water, bay leaf, dried mushrooms and salt and simmer for 30 minutes. Remove from the heat and leave to infuse for 30 minutes.

Make the cider-poached apples. Put the sugar, water, cider and salt into a small saucepan and bring to the boil. Using a parisienne cutter (melon baller) scoop as many balls of apple as you can from each apple, taking care not to get the woody core. Turn the cider mix down to a gentle simmer and add the apple balls. Simmer very gently until just beginning to soften, then remove from the heat and leave to cool.

Once the cider gravy has infused, strain into another saucepan, measure, and bring to the boil. Boil to reduce the sauce to a quarter of its measured volume. Measure the reduction. For every 250ml (8½fl oz/1 cup) of reduction, mix 10g (¼oz/1¼ tbsp) of cornstarch (corn flour) with 20ml (4 tsp) of cold water. Mix the flour paste in and heat gently, stirring to prevent it sticking, until it has thickened. Taste the sauce and adjust the seasoning with salt if needed (see page 15). Keep warm until needed.

Prepare the braised celeriac (celery root). Preheat the oven to (fan) 160°C/180°C/350°F/gas mark 4. Cut the celeriac into 1cm (½-inch) slices, then cut these into neat triangles or squares. Put them into a small casserole pot and pour the measured cider gravy, water and salt over the top. Bake in the oven for 40 minutes until they are almost melting.

At the same time, slice the galette into 1cm (½-inch) slices. Line a baking tray (sheet) with baking parchment and drizzle it with rapeseed oil. Place the slices of potato galette on it so they are covered with oil on the bottom side. Brush the top side generously with rapeseed oil and bake in the oven for 20 minutes. After 20 minutes turn over each slice – you want an even crispy golden brown colouring all over – and bake for another 10 minutes.

Remove the cling film (plastic wrap) from the nut roast, trim off the ends and cut into 1.5cm (½-inch) thick slices. Line a baking tray (sheet) with baking parchment and lay the nut roast slices on it. Drizzle oil over each slice and put into the oven for 25 minutes to warm through and crisp up.

Heat the rapeseed oil for the Brussels sprouts in a wide saucepan and add the sprouts, cut side down, with a generous pinch of salt. Fry until they go a dark golden colour and then add the garlic parsley oil. Toss to evenly cover them and then turn down the heat and gently cook for 2–4 minutes. Remove from the heat and cover the saucepan with a lid or plate so they steam in their own juices for 4 minutes.

Lay 3 slices of nut roast on each of 4 large dinner plates to form a stacked line. Add a piece of potato galette, 2 pieces of braised celeriac, 3 or 4 apple pieces and the Brussels sprouts on each plate. Generously drizzle cider gravy over everything and serve hot.

Fennel and tomatoes, it's the taste of sunshine, of hot summer days and lazy afternoons. The chickpeas (garbanzo beans) take us to the Mediterranean and northern Africa, and the pistachios over the Suez and into the Middle East.

Serves: 4

LEMON BRAISED FENNEL
with Spanish chickpeas (garbanzo beans) in a smoked tomato sauce

FOR THE BRAISED FENNEL
4 fennel bulbs
100ml (3½fl oz/scant ½ cup) extra
    virgin olive oil
2 ripe plum tomatoes
4 lemon zest strips
10ml (2 tsp) lemon juice
150ml (5fl oz/⅔ cup) water
2 star anise
8g (¼oz/1½ tsp) sea salt

FOR THE FENNEL CREAM
200g (7oz) fennel offcuts (from the
    braised fennel, above)
50ml (2fl oz/scant ¼ cup) extra
    virgin olive oil
1 star anise
sea salt
cayenne pepper

FOR THE CHICKPEAS
(GARBANZO BEANS)
400g (14oz) plum tomatoes
50ml (2fl oz/scant ¼ cup) extra
    virgin olive oil, plus extra for
    tomatoes
2 banana shallots, sliced
25ml (1fl oz/5 tsp) high-quality
    extra virgin olive oil
sea salt
cayenne pepper
400g (14oz/2⅔ cups) top-quality
    cooked Spanish chickpeas
    (garbanzo beans) (or canned)

TO SERVE
pistachio pâté (see page 66)
pistachio dukkah (see page 114)
carta di musica (see page 214)

First make the pistachio pâté (see page 66), pistachio dukkah (see page 114) and carta di musica (see page 214).

Preheat the oven to (fan) 140°C/160°C/310°F/gas mark 2½. Trim the fennel stalk and fronds, then cut the fennel lengthways across the middle through the centre of the stem to make "steaks" of fennel held together by the stem. Cut each half into 2 x 1cm (½-inch) slices, so you have 8 thick slices. Reserve the offcuts for the fennel cream.

Heat 60ml (2¼fl oz/¼ cup) of the olive oil in a casserole dish on the hob and add the fennel. Stew gently until the fennel starts to brown. Add the whole tomatoes, lemon zest and juice, measured water, star anise and salt and put the lid on. Put into the oven and leave to stew for 45–60 minutes until the fennel is tender. Remove from the oven and discard the lemon zest and star anise. Drizzle the remaining olive oil over the top, then leave to cool.

Make the fennel cream. Cut the fennel into rough 1cm (½-inch) dice. Gently heat the olive oil in a small saucepan and add the star anise, fennel and a pinch of salt. Turn down the heat and cover with a cartouche (see page 184). Cook very slowly for 30 minutes until very soft. Transfer the contents to a blender and purée until a beautiful creamy consistency. Test for seasoning and add a little cayenne pepper (see page 15).

Make the smoked tomato sauce for the chickpeas (garbanzo beans). Cut the tomatoes in half and toss in a little olive oil. Put 1 tbsp of hickory chips into a stove-top smoker. Place the tomatoes on the smoking grate cut side up. Following the manufacturer's instructions, smoke the tomatoes until cooked with a smoky flavour (see also page 116). Sauté the shallots gently in the regular olive oil until soft but not coloured. Put the shallots and tomatoes into a blender and blend until very smooth. Add the high-quality olive oil and blend briefly to emulsify. Pass through a sieve and season with salt and cayenne pepper (see page 15).

Heat the chickpeas (garbanzo beans) and smoked tomato sauce together in a saucepan gently until hot and thick. At the same, time remove the fennel from its cooking liquid and put into a large frying pan (skillet). Heat gently until it starts to colour, then add about 4 tbsp of the cooking liquid and boil until the liquid has evaporated. Keep warm. Remove the tomatoes from the fennel liquid, cut in half and remove the skins.

Put 2 tablespoons of fennel cream together on each of 4 large plates, spread them out slightly then spread across the plate. Add 2 overlapping slices of pistachio pâté, a piece of fennel and a pile of the tomato and chickpea (garbanzo bean) mix. Then add another piece of fennel and a tomato on top of the chickpea (garbanzo bean) mix. Sprinkle pistachio dukkah over the top and serve hot with carta di musica.

This recipe is a bit of a departure for me as I don't usually cook with the flavours and ingredients of the Far East. Sometimes, however, you get an idea and you just can't shake it. There is no authenticity here, it is simply a delicious plate of food.

Serves: 4

SWEET POTATO & AUBERGINE (EGGPLANT)
with spiced peanut sauce and kimchi

FOR THE PEANUT SAUCE
110g (3¾oz/¾ cup) raw peanuts, preferably without the skin
25ml (1fl oz/5 tsp) peanut oil
50g (1¾oz) shallots, peeled and sliced
4 cloves of garlic, peeled and sliced
5g (⅛oz) organic ginger (see page 60), grated
25ml (1fl oz/5 tsp) water
30g (1¼oz/2 tbsp) brown sugar
10ml (2 tsp) white wine vinegar or rice vinegar
sea salt

FOR THE AUBERGINE (EGGPLANT)
2 large aubergines (eggplants)
10ml (2 tsp) toasted sesame oil
4g (¾ tsp) sea salt

FOR THE SWEET POTATO
3 large sweet potatoes
30ml (1fl oz/2 tbsp) toasted sesame oil
2 large pinches of sea salt

First make the kimchi (see page 101) as it takes 5 days to mature.

Ideally make the peanut sauce a day ahead of serving. Preheat the oven to (fan) 160°C/180°C/350°F/gas mark 4. Put the peanuts onto a baking tray (sheet) and roast for 8–10 minutes until dark. If necessary, remove the skins when cool by rubbing them between your hands. Reserve 10g (¼oz/1 tbsp) of peanuts for the garnish.

Heat the peanut oil in a small saucepan. Add the shallots and fry until just softening, then add the garlic and ginger. Cook until the shallot is soft and the garlic cooked. Add the water, brown sugar and vinegar and cook until the sugar has dissolved but the water hasn't evaporated. Transfer to a blender and add the roasted peanuts. Blend to produce a thick, glossy sauce, adding a little water if needed. Season to taste with salt (see page 15). Store in the fridge for a few hours, or ideally overnight, to thicken.

Put the aubergines (eggplants) into a large steamer and steam for 10–15 minutes until soft but not collapsed. Leave to cool, cut in half, then cut each half down the middle lengthways. Trim to a neat rectangle and cut the skin off the base. Brush the top of each with sesame oil, sprinkle with salt and set aside.

Preheat the oven to (fan) 160°C/180°C/350°F/gas mark 4. Make the sweet potato crisps (see page 28). Take the peanut sauce out of the fridge to come to room temperature.

Trim the ends from the sweet potatoes and cut into 1.5cm (½-inch) slices to give 12 round pieces. Using a vegetable peeler, peel to make round medallion shapes. Place in the centre of a 45cm (18-inch) strip of baking parchment on a baking tray (sheet) and add the sesame oil and salt. Fold the paper over and roll up to create a sealed parcel. Put the sweet potato parcel into the oven and bake for 20–30 minutes until the medallions are soft but not breaking apart (poke through the paper to check).

FOR THE SESAME SEEDS

5g (⅛oz/½ tbsp) seame seeds
10g (¼oz/1 tbsp) roasted peanuts
   (reserved from the peanut sauce)
1 spring onion (scallion), finely
   sliced

FOR THE SPINACH RICE

80g (3oz/⅓ cup) basmati rice
10ml (2 tsp) peanut oil
2 spring onions (scallions), finely
   sliced
400g (14oz/13 cups) spinach
sea salt
4ml (¾ tsp) toasted sesame oil

FOR THE GARNISH

kimchi (see page 101)
sweet potato crisps (see page 28)
1 orange
toasted sesame oil

While the sweet potato is cooking, wash the basmati rice in a small bowl with cold water, drain and repeat. Put the rice, 200ml (7fl oz/generous ¾ cup) of water and 1g (scant ¼ tsp) of salt into a small saucepan and cover with a lid. Simmer gently until the rice is soft and has absorbed all the water. Check for seasoning (see page 15) and keep warm until needed.

Meanwhile, put the sesame seeds on a baking tray (sheet) and roast for 4 minutes. Crush the reserved peanuts and put them and one-third of the spring onions (scallions) into a bowl, then add the hot sesame seeds.

Heat a griddle pan until very hot and 5 minutes before the sweet potato will be cooked, put the aubergine (eggplant) onto the griddle pan cut side down. Don't move it – leave to cook for about 5 minutes.

Heat the peanut oil for the spinach in a saucepan and add the spring onions (scallions). Fry briefly and add the spinach. Stir until wilted, then add a generous pinch of salt. Remove from the heat, add the toasted sesame oil and cooked rice and stir well.

When ready, take the sweet potatoes out of the oven, leave to cool for a few minutes, then remove from the parcel. Carefully remove the aubergine (eggplant) from the griddle.

Place 1–2 tablespoons of peanut suace on each of 4 plates and add 1 piece of aubergine (eggplant), charred side up. Place 2 pieces of sweet potato next to it, leant on top of each other, and add 2 tablespoons of the spinach rice. Take a tablespoon of kimchi and form it into a ball in your hand. Place this next to the spinach, then sprinkle the spring onion (scallion), sesame and peanut mix over the whole plate. Grate a little orange zest and drizzle a little sesame oil over each plate. Lay a sweet potato crisp over the top and serve.

Tagines are a wonderful way of cooking. My sister brought me one back from her honeymoon in Morocco and it spent years sat collecting dust. One day I was stuck for something to cook and decided to give it a go. It was so simple yet the flavours produced inside were a revelation. I don't fully understand the science, but you can't replicate it any other way – casseroles and stew pots just don't have the same effect. This recipe is one of our family favourites, even our 18-month-old son enjoys it at least once a week.

Serves: 4

CARROT, PEA & CARDAMOM TAGINE
with seeded freekeh and flat breads

25ml (1fl oz/5 tsp) extra virgin olive oil

2 onions, sliced

5g (⅛oz/1 tsp) sea salt

5g (⅛oz/2½ tsp) cumin seeds

5g (⅛oz/2½ tsp) coriander seeds, crushed

1 dried red chilli

25g (1oz) organic ginger (see page 60), finely grated

4 cloves of garlic, puréed (see page 147)

12 small shallots, peeled but whole

4 small new potatoes, cut lengthways into quarters

20 baby carrots, trimmed

2g (1 tbsp) saffron

8 cardamom pods

500ml (18fl oz/2 cups) basic stock (see page 64)

150g (5½oz/1 cup) freshly podded peas

50g (1¾oz) sugar snap peas, trimmed and strings removed

15g (½oz/¼ cup) parsley leaves, finely chopped

15g (½oz/generous ½ cup) mint leaves, finely chopped

TO SERVE
seeded freekeh (see page 114)
flat breads (see page 217)

Preheat the oven to (fan) 160°C/180°C/350°F/gas mark 4. Make the seeded freekeh (see page 114) and flat breads (see page 217).

Heat the olive oil gently in a frying pan (skillet), then add the onion and salt and fry for 4 minutes until soft. Add the cumin and coriander seeds and the dried chilli and fry for 1 minute, then add the ginger and garlic. Cook for another 2 minutes and add the shallots and potatoes. Cook for 2 more minutes, then add the carrots, saffron and cardamom pods.

Transfer everything to the tagine and add the stock. Put the lid on the tagine and put it in the oven for 45 minutes. After 30 minutes check the carrots and potatoes. They should be meltingly soft but not broken down. If they are not ready, return to the oven and check every 15 minutes until done. Once done, add the podded peas and return to the oven for 5 minutes.

Remove from the oven and add the sugar snap peas, put the lid on and leave to steam for 30 seconds. Remove the lid and sprinkle the herbs over the top.

Serve the tagine with seeded freekeh and flat breads.

It was my childhood dislike of cauliflower that drove a relentless search for the best possible ways to cook it. In general, I have found the most interesting and satisfying treatments have had an Indian slant.

The slightly bitter edge and the deep sweetness that comes from cooking cauliflower close to burning marries so well with pungent spices. This recipe puts the stem at the heart of the meal and is one of my favourites. Although it takes a little time, it is well worth it. In fact, I'd say that cauliflower is now a contender for one of my favourite vegetables.

Serves: 4

CAULIFLOWER HEARTS
with cauliflower and truffle purée and cauliflower and almond fritters

FOR THE CAULIFLOWER HEARTS
1 very large cauliflower or
  2 medium cauliflowers
rapeseed oil, for frying

FOR THE PURÉES
1 x quantity of kale purée (see
  page 185)
400g (14oz) cauliflower florets
  (reserved from the hearts)
40ml (1½fl oz/8 tsp) extra virgin
  olive oil
sea salt
white truffle oil
water

FOR THE FRITTER FILLING
25 blanched almonds
115g (4oz) cauliflower offcuts from
  the cauliflower hearts (see above)
20ml (4 tsp) rapeseed oil
1g (½ tsp) fenugreek seeds
1g (½ tsp) cumin seeds
small pinch of cayenne pepper
200ml (7fl oz/generous ¾ cup)
  water
0.85g (¼ tsp) agar powder
1.25g (⅓ tsp) iota carrageenan
  powder (or omit the iota
  carrageenan powder and use a
  total of 2g (generous ½ tsp) of
  agar powder)
sea salt

Soak the almonds for the fritters in advance. Place the almonds in a small bowl and cover with water by at least 2cm (¾ inch). Leave for 12 hours, then drain.

Prepare the pickled cauliflower (see page 98) and the kale purée (see page 185).

Cut the stalk and top from the cauliflower, then cut across the cauliflower in half and then cut each half in half again to give 4 discs, each 1–1.5cm (about ½ inch) thick. Using a 7.5cm (3-inch) round cookie cutter, carefully cut out the centre of the cauliflower discs. Reserve the florets and offcuts for the purée and fritters.

Bring 2 litres (3½ pints/8 cups) of water and 30g (1¼oz/1¾ tbsp) of salt to the boil in a large saucepan. Cook the cauliflower hearts for 4–5 minutes until soft but still al dente then shock in ice-cold water (see page 185). Transfer to the fridge.

Preheat the oven to (fan) 160°C/180°C/350°F/gas mark 4.

Toss the cauliflower florets for the purée in the olive oil and a little salt. Place in a baking tin (pan) and roast in the oven for 25 minutes or until golden in colour. Remove from the oven. Weigh the roasted cauliflower and then add 15 per cent of the weight in truffle oil (add 15ml (1 tbsp) of truffle oil for every 100g (3½oz) of cauliflower). Weigh again and calculate 50 per cent of the weight and measure this in water. Add the cauliflower, truffle oil and water to a blender and blend until very smooth, adding a little more water if needed. Taste and adjust the seasoning (see page 15), then chill in the fridge.

Prepare the fritters. Place 8 small, cylindrical moulds on a sheet of baking parchment on a baking tray (sheet). Chop the cauliflower offcuts into 1cm (½-inch) chunks.

Put the rapeseed oil and fenugreek seeds into a frying pan (skillet) and fry gently until they begin to darken but not burn. Add the cumin seeds and cayenne pepper and stir to combine. Add the cauliflower, almonds and measured water and turn down the heat. Stew gently for 15–20 minutes until the cauliflower is completely soft and the water has completely evaporated.

50g (1¾oz/scant ½ cup) gram flour,
    plus extra to coat
40g (1½oz/¼ cup) potato flour
0.3g (large pinch) xanthan gum
5g (⅛oz/1 tsp) caster (superfine)
    sugar
1g (¼ tsp) quick yeast
1g (scant ¼ tsp) sea salt, finely
    ground
150ml (5fl oz/⅔ cup) water at room
    temperature
vegetable oil, for deep-fat frying

TO SERVE

pickled cauliflower (see page 98)
truffle oil
coriander (cilantro) or micro
    coriander (micro cilantro) leaves

Stir in the agar and iota powders. Bring to the boil, then transfer to a blender. Blend until very smooth, then pass through a fine sieve into a jug. Taste and season well with salt (if the fenugreek tastes bitter then add more salt). Pour it quickly into the prepared moulds. Leave for 30 minutes, then transfer to the fridge and leave for 2 hours.

About an hour before serving, make the batter. Mix all the dry ingredients together in a bowl, then add the water and whisk to form a batter. Leave somewhere warm for an hour. Take the roasted cauliflower purée and the kale purée out of the fridge 1 hour before needed to come to room temperature. Take the pickled cauliflower out of the fridge and drain away all the liquid.

Preheat the oven to (fan) 160°C/180°C/350°F/gas mark 4. Line a small baking tray (sheet) with baking parchment. Prepare your deep-fat fryer (see page 26).

Heat a little rapeseed oil in the bottom of a large frying pan (skillet). Add the cauliflower hearts and fry on a high heat until golden brown. Remove from the pan, put onto the prepared tray and keep warm in the oven.

The curried cauliflower and almond fritters will only keep for 4 minutes when cooked so only do the following once everything else is ready. Remove the fritters from the moulds. Whisk the batter with a fork to knock the bubbles out of it. Toss the fritters in gram flour to coat, then place into the batter mix. Using a fork, lower each fritter into the hot oil. Shake the pan gently to prevent it sticking to the bottom and repeat with each fritter, taking care not to let them stick to each other (you may need to do this in batches). When golden brown, remove and drain on kitchen (paper) towel.

To serve, drizzle a spoonful of the kale purée around the edge of each plate. Put a spoonful of roasted cauliflower and truffle purée in the centre of each plate and drag it with the back of a spoon. Place the cauliflower heart and cauliflower almond fritter on top of the purée. Drizzle a little truffle oil over the top and then add a few coriander (cilantro) leaves. Scatter 8 pieces of pickled cauliflower around and serve it all together while still warm.

THE MAILLARD REACTION

The Maillard reaction is the complex chemical interaction between proteins and sugars in a foodstuff when exposed to a high, direct heat source. Think of the brown bits on roast potatoes, the deep flavour of fried onions, or the texture of crispy cabbage – it is the Maillard reaction that results in the browning of vegetables and leads to a complex satisfying flavour.

No vegetable demonstrates the importance of the Maillard reaction in cooking vegetables as well as the cauliflower. When you boil cauliflower you are dissolving the natural sugars and nutrients into the water, thus making it less sweet and nutritious, as well as breaking down the cell walls and releasing all the sulphurous, cabbage flavours.

Applying a direct, high, heat source, such as sautéing, to completely dry cauliflower, until a deep golden brown colour, encourages the sugars and proteins in the cauliflower to react and create a complex, biscuity flavour that is magical. The key here is colour: you want a deep golden brown on as much of the surface as possible – too light and no magic will have taken place (it will just taste like boiled cauliflower); too dark and it will be burnt because the molecules will have interacted to the point of destruction.

I love the flavour of roasted winter squash. It has a deep, sweet umami (see page 16) and a wonderful colour, it's just a shame about the texture. The more you roast it, the better the flavour, but the more mushy the texture becomes. Slicing it very finely and setting it in a terrine is my solution to this problem as you get the soft bite of the multiple layers combined with the wonderful depth of flavour that comes from slow cooking in the oven. This recipe will make more terrine than you need, but you can either double up on the portions or save it for an elegant lunch with bread and a nice green salad.

Serves: 4

PRESSED WINTER SQUASH
with cavolo nero, smoked hazelnut milk and rye grain

FOR THE RYE GRAIN

80g (2¾oz/½ cup) rye grain
pinch of salt
1 x quantity of smoked hazelnut milk (see page 221)

FOR THE PRESSED SQUASH

300g (10½oz) peeled and deseeded butternut squash
600g (1lb 5oz) peeled and deseeded muscat de provence squash
10g (¼oz/1¾ tsp) sea salt
50g (1¾oz/¼ cup) caster (superfine) sugar
1 clove of garlic, puréed (see page 147)
2.5g (3 tsp) sage leaves, sliced
1.5g (¾ tsp) grated lemon zest
4g (1¼ tsp) agar powder
drizzle of hazelnut oil

FOR THE PICKLED SQUASH

12 slices of butternut squash
50ml (2fl oz/scant ¼ cup) cider vinegar
50g (1¾oz/¼ cup) caster (superfine) sugar
150ml (5fl oz/⅔ cup) water
5g (⅛oz/1 tsp) sea salt

Put the rye grain into a bowl and completely cover in cold water. Soak for at least 4 hours. When soaked, drain and rinse and put into a small saucepan, cover with water and add a pinch of salt. Boil gently for about 30 minutes until the grain is soft but with a "pop". Drain and set aside.

Prepare the smoked hazelnut milk (see page 221). Prepare the cavolo nero purée (see page 185). Line a 900g (2lb) loaf tin (pan) with baking parchment.

Cut 12 x 1mm thin, round slices of butternut from the top of the butternut squash for the pickled squash and set aside. Cut the rest of the butternut squash into very thin slices on a mandolin. Do the same for the muscat squash. Weigh out the correct amount of each squash and place in a large bowl, reserving the rest of the squash for the purée. Mix the salt and sugar together and mix with the squash slices. Set aside for 30 minutes.

Make the pickled squash. Place the vinegar, sugar, water and salt in a saucepan and heat until boiling. Add the 12 slices of butternut squash and simmer for 3–5 minutes until soft, then remove from the heat and allow to cool in the liquid.

Make the pressed squash. Mix together the garlic, sage and lemon zest, then add to the muscat and butternut squash. Sprinkle the agar over the top and mix to combine. Preheat the oven to (fan) 160°C/180°C/350°F/gas mark 4.

Layer the squash slices in the prepared loaf tin (pan), pressing down to ensure even density. Once all the squash is in, push down again to compact. Cover in a sheet of baking parchment and then wrap very tightly in foil to seal. Bake in the oven for 45–60 minutes.

While the terrine is cooking, make the squash purée. Place a piece of baking parchment 45cm (18 inches) long on a baking tray (sheet). Place the squash in the middle, add the olive oil and salt, then roll up the baking parchment to form a sealed parcel. Bake in the oven for 25 minutes until the squash is soft. Remove from the oven, allow to cool for 5 minutes, then transfer the contents to a blender along with the hazelnut oil. Blend until very smooth and then taste and adjust the seasoning if necessary (see page 15). Set aside.

FOR THE PURÉES

5 tbsp cavolo nero purée (see page 185)

250g (9oz) squash (reserved from the offcuts from the terrine, cut into equal-sized chunks)

10ml (2tsp) extra virgin olive oil

1g (scant ¼ tsp) sea salt

15ml (1 tbsp) hazelnut oil

FOR THE GARNISH

4 cavolo nero leaves, stems removed

hazelnut oil, to drizzle

Stick a cocktail stick through the terrine foil into the squash to test if it is done. When it is ready it should meet no resistance. If you feel it click through the layers, put it back into the oven in 10-minute bursts until ready. When ready, remove from the oven and, using another loaf tin (pan) or similar, press down on the terrine to compress the squash. Leave the empty tin (pan) in place and fill it with a full jam jar or similar weight. Leave on a cooling rack until cold, then remove the weights and put the terrine into the fridge for 1 hour.

When chilled, remove from the fridge and remove the foil. Turn the tin (pan) out, remove the paper liner and trim the edges to a neat rectangle. Cut widthways into neat slices about 1.5cm (½ inch) across. Line a baking tray (sheet) with baking parchment and arrange the 4 pressed squash slices on it. Put into the oven for 10 minutes to reheat.

Take each of the 12 slices of pickled squash and cut from the centre straight out to one edge. Lift one cut side over the other and twist it round to form a cone. Put these to one side for garnish.

Put the cavolo nero purée into a small saucepan with 1 tsp of water and heat through gently. At the same time, put the rye grain in a small saucepan and just cover with the smoked hazelnut milk. Bring to a simmer and cook gently to thicken to a risotto consistency.

Meanwhile, blanch the cavolo nero leaves for 3 minutes, then shock in ice-cold water (see page 185).

Remove the pressed squash from the oven and drizzle each piece with hazelnut oil to give it a glossy sheen. Place 1 slice on each of 4 plates. Lay 1 strip of blanched cavolo nero leaf next to each slice and place a spoonful of the cavolo nero purée on top. Fold it over to contain the purée and then add a pile of the hazelnut rye mix next to it and add 2 tablespoons of squash purée. Arrange 3 pickled squash cones around the plate and drizzle a little hazelnut oil over the top. Serve immediately.

| PURÉES |

I make a lot of purées ... and I mean a lot of purées. They are a great way to use offcuts of vegetables and they bring a lovely, vibrant colour and a creamy texture that can help to lift a dish from a few nice things on a plate to a true eating experience.

ASPARAGUS & HERB PURÉE

Makes: 4 portions

250g (9oz) asparagus
75ml (2¾fl oz/⅓ cup) extra virgin olive oil
100g (3½oz) onion, sliced
25g (1oz/scant 1 cup) spinach
5g (⅛oz/2 tbsp) chopped parsley leaves
2g (2 tsp) tarragon leaves
200ml (7fl oz/generous ¾ cup) cold water
sea salt

Cut the asparagus stems into 5mm (¼-inch) slices, discarding the tough, woody ends.

Heat 25ml (1fl oz/5 tsp) of the olive oil in a large saucepan and add the onion. Simmer gently until the onion is beginning to soften, then add the asparagus. Cook until soft but still green, then add the spinach, parsley and tarragon. Stir and cook until the spinach leaves have just wilted.

Transfer to a blender, add the measured water and remaining olive oil and blend until the purée is completely smooth. Season to taste (see page 15). Pass through a sieve and put straight into a container, covered with cling film (plastic wrap) in contact with the purée, to cool quickly.

This will keep in the fridge for up to 2 days.

CHERVIL PURÉE

Makes: 4 portions

50g (1¾oz/generous ¾ cup) chervil leaves
50g (1¾oz /generous ¾ cup) parsley leaves
105ml (3½fl oz/scant ½ cup) extra virgin olive oil
75g (2¾oz) shallots, sliced
100g (3½oz/3⅓ cups) spinach
10ml (2 tsp) black truffle oil
sea salt

Put a small metal baking tin (pan) in the freezer to chill. Blanch the chervil and parsley for about 90 seconds, until a vibrant green colour, then shock in ice-cold water (see page 185). Remove the herbs from the water and squeeze dry. Chop roughly and set aside.

Heat 30ml (1fl oz/2 tbsp) of the olive oil in a frying pan (skillet) and add the shallots. Cook until just soft, then add the spinach. Cook briefly until wilted, then remove from the heat.

Put the shallots and spinach into a blender along with the blanched herbs and remaining olive oil. Blend for at least 4 minutes until silky smooth (you may need to add a little water). Add the truffle oil and season with salt to taste (see page 15). Remove the baking tin (pan) from the freezer and pour the herb purée onto it. Place a sheet of cling film (plastic wrap) tightly against the surface of the purée and refrigerate.

This will keep in the fridge for up to 2 days.

PARSNIP & SHALLOT PURÉE

Makes: 4 portions

25g (1oz/scant ¼ cup) smoked hazelnuts (see page 116)
20ml (4 tsp) extra virgin olive oil
75g (2¾oz) banana shallots, sliced
225g (8oz) parsnips, peeled, trimmed and cut into
   2mm (¹⁄₁₆ inch) slices
250ml (8½fl oz/1 cup) water
15ml (1 tbsp) hazelnut oil

Make the smoked hazelnuts (see page 116).

Heat the olive oil in a large saucepan until just hot, then add the shallots. Cook gently until just soft, then add the parsnip. Cook gently for 2 minutes, then add the water and simmer for 15–20 minutes until soft.

Transfer the shallot and parsnip mix into a blender and add the hazelnut oil and smoked hazelnuts. Process until very smooth, adding just a little water if needed, to make a thick, silky purée.

This will keep in the fridge for up to 3 days.

BROAD BEAN (FAVA BEAN) PURÉE

Makes: 4 portions

50g (1¾oz/⅓ cup) split dried broad beans (fava beans)
25ml (1fl oz/5 tsp) extra virgin olive oil
2 cloves of garlic, thinly sliced
75ml (2¾fl oz/⅓ cup) water
sea salt
cayenne pepper

Put the dried broad beans (fava beans) into a small bowl and cover with cold water by at least 2cm (¾ inch). Soak for at least 4 hours or ideally overnight. Strain and rinse in cold water.

Put the beans into a small saucepan and add 500ml (18fl oz/ 2 cups) of cold water. Bring to the boil and simmer very gently until the beans are cooked but not breaking up.

Put the olive oil into a small saucepan and heat gently. Add the garlic and cook until soft but not coloured. Add the broad beans (fava beans) and measured water and bring to the boil. As soon as it boils, transfer to a blender and blend until smooth. Season with salt and cayenne pepper to taste (see page 15).

This will keep in the fridge for up to 3 days.

CARTOUCHE

Sometimes you want to cover something in a saucepan to slow down the evaporation of liquids and aromatic compounds, but a lid will be too efficient at the job. Using a cartouche is a wonderful way of keeping a succulent stewed texture but allowing a little liquid to evaporate naturally. It is simply a round piece of baking parchment the size of the saucepan you are using, with a small hole in the middle, which is pushed down on top of the ingredients being cooked.

KALE PURÉE

Makes: 4 portions

100g (3½oz) kale, stems removed
20ml (4 tsp) extra virgin olive oil
25–75ml (1–2¾fl oz/5 tsp–⅓ cup) water
sea salt

Blanch the kale and then shock in ice-cold water (see box, below). Remove from the water and squeeze out any liquid. Chop the kale roughly, then put in a blender with the olive oil and a little water, starting with 25ml (1fl oz/5 tsp). Blend to a very smooth purée, adding a little more water if needed. Pass through a sieve and season with salt to taste.

This will keep in the fridge for up to 3 days.

CAVOLO NERO PURÉE

Makes: 4 portions

100g (3½oz) cavolo nero leaves, stems removed
1 clove of garlic
30ml (1fl oz/2 tbsp) extra virgin olive oil
sea salt

Blanch the cavolo nero and garlic for 3 minutes, then shock in ice-cold water (see box, opposite). Remove from the water and squeeze out any excess liquid to make a ball. Chop roughly, then put in a blender. Add the olive oil and process to a coarse paste. Season to taste with salt (see page 15).

This will keep in the fridge for up to 3 days.

SUNFLOWER SEED PURÉE

Makes: 4 portions

200g (7oz/1½ cups) sunflower seeds
20g (¾oz/1⅔ tbsp) caster (superfine) sugar
20ml (4 tsp) sunflower oil
200ml (7fl oz/generous ¾ cup) water
sea salt
cayenne pepper

Preheat the oven to (fan) 160°C/180°C/350°F/gas mark 4.

Put the sunflower seeds on a baking tray (sheet) and bake in the oven for 10 minutes until a dark brown colour. Transfer the seeds to a blender with the sugar, oil and water and blend until very smooth. Taste and season with salt and cayenne pepper (see page 15).

This will keep in the fridge for up to 3 days.

BLANCHING AND SHOCKING GREEN VEGETABLES

Keeping your green vegetables green is an important skill to master. It is relatively simple, you just need to remember a few principles:

1. *Have your water at boiling point when you add your vegetables.*
2. *You need a lot of water, so when your greens are added the water doesn't stop boiling and they cook as quickly as possible.*
3. *Add 1.5 per cent of salt to the volume of your water, so for 4 litres (7 pints/16 cups) of water add 60g (2oz/3½ tbsp) of salt (any kind of salt).*
4. *Have a lot of ice-cold water to plunge your greens into once cooked, so the cooking stops instantly and their temperature drops as quickly as possible.*
5. *Don't leave your greens in the cold water once chilled. As soon as they are cold, remove them from the water.*
6. *Keep your blanched greens away from any source of acid until ready to serve or you will risk having a grey/yellow mess just when you want them to look their best.*

DESSERTS

This has become something of a classic at the restaurant, it is so simple to look at, the flavours so familiar, but nothing can prepare you for the intensity and clarity of the flavours. Using as few ingredients as possible in each element allows the purity of the ingredients to shine through – the peanuts taste purely of peanuts, the chocolate and caramel exactly of that. Just remember that the sorbet and the tart need four to five hours to set.

Serves: 8

CHOCOLATE SALTED CARAMEL TART
with peanut butter sorbet

FOR THE SORBET
70g (2½oz/⅓ cup) caster (superfine) sugar
0.5g (scant ¼ tsp) xanthan gum
175ml (6fl oz/¾ cup) cold water
175ml (6fl oz/¾ cup) glucose syrup
150g (5½oz) unsweetened crunchy peanut butter
25ml (1fl oz/5 tsp) brandy

FOR THE TART BASE
90g (3oz/¾ cup) plain (all-purpose) flour
10g (¼oz/1¼ tbsp) cornflour (cornstarch)
20g (¾oz/1⅔ tbsp) caster (superfine) sugar
pinch of salt
30ml (1fl oz/2 tbsp) extra virgin olive oil
20ml (4 tsp) cold water
25g (1oz) dark chocolate, 53% cocoa solids

FOR THE TART FILLING
400g (14oz) dark chocolate, 53% cocoa solids, finely chopped or coarsely grated
7g (¼oz/1¼ tsp) sea salt
125g (4½oz/⅔ cup) caster (superfine) sugar
300ml (10fl oz/1¼ cups) cold water

To serve
4 tsp cocoa nibs

Make the sorbet first. Mix the sugar and xanthan together. Place the measured water in a large saucepan, then whisk in the sugar and xanthan. Add the glucose syrup and peanut butter and bring to the boil. Immediately remove from the heat and add the brandy. Allow the sorbet to cool slightly, then put into an ice-cream machine and follow the manufacturer's instructions before freezing. Or see making sorbets by hand on page 201.

Preheat the oven to (fan) 160°C/180°C/350°F/gas mark 4.

Mix all the ingredients for the tart base together, except for the dark chocolate, in a large bowl to form a dough. Place the dough between 2 sheets of baking parchment and roll it out until 1mm thick (very thin). Refrigerate for 30 minutes.

Put the dough on a large baking tray (sheet), leaving the top sheet of baking parchment on, and bake for 15–25 minutes until just crisp. Remove from the oven and remove the baking parchment. While still hot, place the base of a 21cm (8-inch) springform cake tin (pan) onto the pastry and cut round it. Return the base to the springform tin (pan) and line with baking parchment. Fit the cut pastry base inside. Place the dark chocolate for the tart base in a bain-marie (see box, below) and melt gently. Spread evenly over the pastry base.

Make the tart filling. Place the chocolate and salt in an electric mixer fitted with a whisk attachment. Put the sugar into a small, heavy-based saucepan and gently melt until it becomes a dark caramel. Add the water and simmer until the sugar has melted.

Weigh out 250g (9oz) of the boiling caramel and pour over the chocolate and salt in the electric mixer. Whisk on the lowest speed until the temperature has reduced to 27°C/80°F. Pour the mix onto the base and put in the fridge for 4–5 hours to set.

Remove the chocolate tart from the fridge and from the tin (pan) – use a blowtorch to gently heat the outside if necessary. Cut into slices and place 1 slice on each plate. Place 1 tsp of cocoa nibs next to the tart and top with a quenelle of sorbet.

> ### BAIN-MARIE
> *Make a bain-marie, or water bath, by setting a heatproof bowl over a small saucepan filled with 2cm (¾ inch) of boiling water. Turn the heat down so the water is just simmering and add the ingredient you wish to melt to the heatproof bowl.*

I love how simple this looks, just a mousse with a chocolate tuille on top, but if made perfectly you will be blown away by the textures and contrast between the rich, smooth chocolatey mousse and the sharp yet sweet passion fruit gel hidden in the middle. You do need to make this in advance to allow time to set. Alternatively, just make the mousse for a quick, easy dessert.

Serves: 4

CHOCOLATE MOUSSE
with passion fruit gel and a chocolate tuille

FOR THE GEL

50g (1¾oz/¼ cup) caster (superfine) sugar

4g (1¼ tsp) agar powder

1.2g (½ tsp) xanthan gum

200ml (7fl oz/generous ¾ cup) water

100g (3½oz) passion fruit flesh (from about 6 passion fruits)

20ml (4 tsp) lemon juice

FOR THE MOUSSE

100ml (3½fl oz/scant ½ cup) unsalted aquafaba (see page 76)

15g (½oz/1¼ tbsp) caster (superfine) sugar

1g (scant ¼ tsp) sea salt

100g (3½oz) dark chocolate, 70% cocoa solids

50ml (2fl oz/scant ¼ cup) boiling water

FOR THE TUILLES

5g (⅛oz/⅔ tbsp) cornflour (cornstarch)

10g (¼oz/2 tbsp) cocoa powder

25g (1oz/2 tbsp) caster (superfine) sugar

10ml (2 tsp) water

Make the gel first. Mix the sugar, agar and xanthan together. Put the water into a small saucepan and whisk in the sugar mix. Slowly heat until it just begins to boil, whisking the whole time. As soon as it boils, remove from the heat and whisk in the passion fruit. Pass through a sieve into a bowl, then leave in the fridge for 1 hour to set to a hard jelly. Transfer the jelly to a blender, add the lemon juice, and blend to a smooth gel, adding a little water if necessary. Spoon the gel into 4 tall moulds, each 2cm (¾ inch) in diameter. Make sure they are 3cm (1¼ inches) full, then put in the freezer for 5 hours.

When the gel is ready, seal the bottom of 4 x 5cm (2-inch) diameter ring moulds with cling film (plastic wrap) and make the mousse. Put the aquafaba into a clean bowl and whisk to stiff peaks. Mix the sugar and salt together and add to the aquafaba, a sprinkle at a time, whisking continuously and maintaining stiff peaks. Set aside.

Put the chocolate into a heatproof bowl and add the measured boiling water. Stir to melt, then put over a bain-marie (see page 188) until completely melted. Place the bowl in cold water to cool the chocolate, stirring until it reaches 35–40°C (95–104°F). Check the aquafaba meringue is still firm, and if necessary whisk back to stiff peaks. Add one-third of the meringue mix to the chocolate. Stir quickly and gently to mix. Add a further third of the meringue and fold it in. Then add the rest of the meringue and gently fold it in.

Remove the frozen gel cylinders from the freezer, warm the outside of the mould and pop out the cylinders. Fill your moulds two-thirds full with chocolate mousse and gently push a frozen gel cylinder into each one, making sure it doesn't sink to the bottom. Add the rest of the mousse on top and level off. Put in the fridge for 12 hours to set.

To make the tuilles, preheat the oven to (fan) 160°C/180°C/350°F/gas mark 4. Line a large baking tray (sheet) with non-stick baking parchment. Put the cornflour (cornstarch), cocoa and sugar in a small bowl and mix to remove any lumps. Add the water and mix to a paste. Put 1 small teaspoon of mix onto the prepared tray and spread it out as thinly as you can. Leaving a space of 2cm (¾ inch) between each tuille, keep making the tuilles until the mix is finished. Bake in the oven for 5–10 minutes, checking every few minutes to make sure they don't burn. When they stop bubbling, remove from the oven and leave until cold – they will become brittle and glassy.

When ready to serve, remove the cling film (plastic wrap) and warm the ring slightly to remove the mousse. Place on a dessert plate, add a chocolate tuille on top and serve.

You've probably come across strawberries with basil and black pepper before, it's such a good combination that it no longer appears that innovative. This dish takes flavours that normally form a savoury salad and ups the sweetness to balance the strawberries and therefore make a lovely dessert instead. This recipe makes 8 parfaits, but they keep well in the freezer. Allow up to 8 hours for the parfait to set and 4 hours for the strawberries to macerate.

Serves: 4

MACERATED STRAWBERRIES
with pine nut parfait and thyme meringues

FOR THE PARFAIT
50g (1¾oz/⅓ cup) pine nuts
75g (2¾oz/½ cup) cashew nuts
15ml (3 tsp) lemon juice
0.35g (scant ¼ tsp) lemon zest
75ml (2¾fl oz/⅓ cup) water
125g (4½oz/⅔ cup) caster
    (superfine) sugar
25ml (1fl oz/5 tsp) glucose syrup
4g (¾ tsp) sea salt
1g (⅓ tsp) xanthan gum
150g (5½oz/⅔ cup) fridge-cold
    coconut cream
50ml (2fl oz/scant ¼ cup) aquafaba
    (see page 76)
50g (1¾oz/¼ cup) caster
    (superfine) sugar

FOR THE MERINGUES
50ml (2fl oz/scant ¼ cup) aquafaba
    (see page 76)
1g (scant ¼ tsp) sea salt
50g (1¾oz/¼ cup) caster
    (superfine) sugar
2g (2½ tsp) thyme leaves
freshly ground black pepper

FOR THE STRAWBERRIES
200g (7oz) ripe strawberries
20g (¾oz/1⅔ tbsp) caster
    (superfine) sugar
10ml (2 tsp) lemon juice
4 tbsp good, peppery olive oil

FOR DECORATION
24 small basil leaves
handful of toasted pine nuts

Preheat the oven to (fan) 160°C/180°C/350°F/gas mark 4. Prepare 8 x 4cm (1½-inch) moulds. Wrap the bases in cling film (plastic wrap) and place on a baking tray (sheet). Make the parfait. Put the pine nuts and cashews onto a baking tray (sheet) and toast in the oven for 5 minutes. Add to a blender with the lemon juice and zest, the water, sugar, glucose syrup, salt and xanthan. Blend until very smooth, then pass through a sieve into a mixing bowl. Place in the fridge, covered with cling film (plastic wrap), to firm up for 20 minutes.

Put the coconut cream into a bowl and, using a wire whisk, whisk until it forms stiff peaks. Add a third of the coconut cream to the pine nut mix and stir it in. Add a further third and fold it in gently, then add the remaining third and fold it in carefully. Return the mix to the fridge while you prepare the aquafaba.

Put the aquafaba for the parfait into a clean bowl and whisk to soft peaks. Add the sugar 2 tbsp at a time and whisk until all the sugar is incorporated and it is glossy and holds stiff peaks. Add a third of the mix to the pine nut mix and stir it in. Add a further third and fold it in, then add the last third and fold it in. Spoon the parfait into your moulds and freeze for 4–8 hours.

Make the meringues. Ideally use a dehydrator set to 60°C/140°F. If using the oven, preheat to its lowest setting. Line a dehydrator tray or baking tray (sheet) with baking parchment. Put the aquafaba and salt into a clean mixing bowl and whisk to form stiff peaks. Add the sugar 1 tbsp at a time and whisk in before adding more. Continue until all the sugar is incorporated and you have stiff peaks. Fold the thyme leaves in and transfer to a piping bag. Pipe 1cm (½-inch) meringues onto the tray. Grind black pepper over the top and bake in the dehydrator or oven for 4–8 hours or until dry and crisp all the way through. Quarter the strawberries, put into a bowl and toss in the sugar and lemon juice. Cover the bowl with cling film (plastic wrap) and put into the fridge for 4 hours.

When ready, spoon most of the macerated strawberries out of their liquid (keeping some for garnish) onto kitchen (paper) towel to dry. In a small bowl, mix 4 tablespoons of the strawberry juice with the olive oil. Remove 4 parfaits from the freezer and warm in your hands until the parfait comes loose. Place 1 parfait on each of 4 dessert plates and pile a quarter of the macerated strawberries next to it. Add about 6 small basil leaves and dress the strawberries with the strawberry and olive oil mix. Scatter a few pine nuts on top and add 4–5 meringues to each plate. Serve immediately.

Peaches and prosecco are at the heart of a Bellini cocktail. However, it is a little sickly sweet for my taste. This recipe burns the sugars in the peach to give a more complex experience and uses a touch of lemon thyme to add a herbaceous lemony tinge. You need four hours for the sorbet to set and at least four hours for the peaches to macerate.

Serves: 4

BURNT PEACHES
with prosecco sorbet and almond biscotti

FOR THE PEACHES
4 yellow-fleshed peaches, ripe but
    firm, halved and stones removed
caster (superfine) sugar
4 sprigs of lemon thyme

FOR THE SORBET
225g (8oz/1⅛ cups) caster
    (superfine) sugar
225ml (7½fl oz/scant 1 cup) water
300ml (10floz/1¼ cups) prosecco
90ml (3¼fl oz/generous ⅓ cup)
    lemon juice

FOR THE BISCOTTI
75g (2¾oz/½ cup) almonds
100g (3½oz/¾ cup) plain
    (all-purpose) flour
100g (3½oz/½ cup) caster
    (superfine) sugar
2.5g (½ tsp) baking powder
twist of grated nutmeg
zest of ½ lemon
50ml (2fl oz/scant ¼ cup) cold
    water

FOR DECORATION
4 sprigs of lemon thyme leaves,
    picked

Slice a little off the back of the peaches to give a flat surface. Weigh the peaches and measure 20 per cent of their weight in sugar (for 500g (1lb 2oz) of peaches weigh 100g (3½oz/½ cup) of sugar). Put the peaches and sugar into a bowl and mix well. Leave for at least 4 hours, or overnight in the fridge.

Make the sorbet. Put the sugar and water into a small lidded saucepan and heat until the sugar dissolves, ideally without boiling. Remove from the heat and allow to cool completely, then mix in the prosecco and lemon juice. If using an ice-cream maker, follow the manufacturer's instructions then store in the freezer. Otherwise see making sorbets by hand on page 201.

Make the biscotti. Preheat the oven to (fan) 160°C/180°C/350°F/gas mark 4. Line a large baking tray (sheet) with non-stick baking parchment. In a blender, process half the almonds until coarsely crushed then mix with the whole almonds and the rest of the ingredients except the water. Add the water and bring together into a dough. Roll the dough into a log 4cm (1½ inches) in diameter. Place the log on the baking tray (sheet) and bake in the oven for 25 minutes or until light brown. Remove from the oven, allow to cool, then slice into 1cm (½-inch) slices.

Re-line the baking tray (sheet) and lay the biscotti out. Turn the oven down to (fan) 140°C/160°C/310°F/gas mark 2½ and put the biscotti back into the oven for 10–15 minutes. Remove from the oven and allow to cool completely – they should be hard and crunchy once cool. Place 3 biscotti in a food processor and pulse to coarse crumbs.

Remove the peaches from their macerating liquid and pat dry with kitchen (paper) towel. Line a large frying pan (skillet) with non-stick baking parchment and heat until searing hot. Add the peaches, cut side down, along with the lemon thyme. Cook until completely caramelized and burnt in appearance. Flip over and repeat on the other side. Remove from the heat and place 2 slices, cut side up, on each of 4 dessert plates.

Add a little pile of biscotti to each plate, scoop a large ball of sorbet on top, and add 2 biscotti. Scatter the thyme leaves over the top and serve straight away.

This dessert is really a fancy Bakewell tart. I didn't mean to create it that way; it was only when I put it together on the plate that it clicked. I wanted to make a beautiful almond and olive oil slice using artisan techniques and I came up with this frangipane-like creation that has a really moreish quality. It's great with a cup of coffee in the morning, but to form a dessert it needed something to cut through it and raspberries were the obvious choice. It turns out it was obvious because it is one of the classic English desserts. So much for originality!

Serves: 8

ALMOND SPONGE
with raspberry and vodka sorbet

FOR THE GRAM FLOUR FERMENT
60g (2oz/½ cup) gram flour
90ml (3¼fl oz/generous ⅓ cup) water

FOR THE SORBET
450g (1lb/3⅔ cups) raspberries (fresh or frozen)
150g (5½oz/¾ cup) caster (superfine) sugar
100ml (3½fl oz/scant ½ cup) glucose syrup
200ml (7fl oz/generous ¾ cup) water
50ml (2fl oz/scant ¼ cup) vodka
1g (⅓ tsp) xanthan gum

FOR THE SPONGE
125g (4½oz/1 cup) plain (all-purpose) flour
75g (2¾oz/⅔ cup) ground almonds
5g (⅛ oz/1 tsp) baking powder
150g (5½oz) gram flour ferment (see above)
200g (7oz/1 cup) caster (superfine) sugar
3ml (generous ½ tsp) almond extract
3g (½ tsp) sea salt
125ml (4fl oz/½ cup) extra virgin olive oil
15g (½oz/2½ tbsp) flaked almonds

FOR DECORATION
16 toasted blanched almonds

First make the gram flour ferment as it needs 24 hours to ferment. Sieve the gram flour, then put it into a small clean jar and add the water. Mix together to form a smooth paste. Cover the jar with a piece of muslin (cheesecloth) or kitchen (paper) towel and fasten using string or an elastic band. Leave in a warm place (23–26°C/73–79°F) for a minimum of 8 hours, an optimum of 24 hours, and a maximum of 48 hours.

Make the sorbet in advance so it can set. Put the raspberries, sugar, glucose syrup and water in a saucepan and cover with a lid. Gently bring to the boil and simmer, stirring occasionally, for about 5 minutes. Transfer to a blender with the vodka and xanthan and blend until smooth. Sieve into a bowl and allow to cool. Transfer to an ice-cream maker and follow the manufacturer's instructions, then store in the freezer. Otherwise see making sorbets by hand on page 201.

When ready to make the cake, check the gram flour ferment – the mix should appear bubbly. Preheat the oven to (fan) 140°C/160°C/310°F/gas mark 2½. Grease and line a 21cm (8-inch) springform cake tin (pan) with baking parchment.

Mix the flour, ground almonds and baking powder together in a bowl. Put the meaured gram flour ferment, sugar, almond extract and salt together in another bowl and whisk until the sugar has dissolved. Slowly add the oil to emulsify. If it starts to split add 1 tbsp of the flour mix. Once all the oil is incorporated, add the flour in 3 batches and stir gently until mixed. Transfer to the prepared cake tin (pan) and scatter the flaked almonds over the top. Bake in the oven for 40 minutes. When cooked it should be golden brown and the middle should no longer wobble.

Remove the tin (pan) and let the cake cool completely on a wire rack. Chop the toasted almonds into a coarse crumb. Cut 8 slices of almond cake and place a slice on each of 8 dessert plates. Place a little pile of chopped almonds next to each slice of cake and top with a scoop of sorbet. Serve before the sorbet melts.

This frozen olive oil dessert is a miracle. It is rich, buttery and moreish. Even if you don't like pineapple it is worth making the semi-freddo. Sometimes I serve it with a tomato salad as a starter, sometimes with strawberries. Pineapple and anise flavours are a match made in heaven, and the olive oil's richness is the perfect accompaniment.

Serves: 4

SPICED PINEAPPLE
with candied fennel and olive oil semi-freddo

FOR THE SEMI-FREDDO
175g (6¼oz/generous ¾ cup) caster (superfine) sugar
5g (⅛oz/2 tsp) soy lecithin
1g (⅓ tsp) xanthan gum
3g (½ tsp) sea salt
150ml (5fl oz/⅔ cup) water
15ml (1 tbsp) pernod (or vodka)
125ml (4fl oz/½ cup) grassy Sicilian olive oil

FOR THE FENNEL
50g (1¾oz/¼ cup) caster (superfine) sugar
1 star anise
150ml (5fl oz/⅔ cup) water
2 vanilla pods, cut in half and seeds scraped
50ml (2fl oz/scant ¼ cup) lemon juice
1 head fennel, stalk and outer layers removed

FOR THE POACHED PINEAPPLE
1 large pineapple
300ml (10fl oz/1¼ cups) water
100g (3½oz/½ cup) caster (superfine) sugar
1 star anise

FOR DECORATION
pineapple (reserved from above)
candied fennel seeds (see page 116)
20g (¾oz/scant 1 cup) basil leaves, shredded
10g (¼oz/generous ⅓ cup) mint leaves, finely sliced

Make the semi-freddo a day before serving so it can set. Mix the sugar, soy lecithin, xanthan and salt together in a bowl. Put the water in a saucepan and whisk in the sugar mix, bit by bit. Gently heat without boiling and stir until the sugar dissolves. Remove from the heat, cover with a lid and leave to cool completely. Transfer to a blender with the pernod and turn on just enough to form a vortex. Slowly pour in the olive oil as if making an aioli (see page 38). Keep adding the oil very slowly to emulsify. When all the mix has been incorporated put into an ice-cream maker and follow the manufacturer's instructions. (Or put in the freezer and whisk by hand every 30 minutes until a softly whipped cream consistency.) Freeze in a pre-chilled container lined with cling film (plastic wrap) for at least 4 hours.

Prepare the fennel at least 4 hours before serving. Put the sugar, star anise and measured water into a small saucepan and heat gently until the sugar dissolves. Add the vanilla seeds and lemon juice, then put in the fridge to chill until icy cold. Cut across the base of the fennel to reveal a flat, wide area, then cut into paper-thin wafers on a mandolin. Put the fennel slices into the prepared sugar syrup and leave for 4 hours.

Make the candied fennel seeds (see page 116).

Remove the pineapple skin then cut the flesh into quarters lengthways. Cut out the core and cut 2 of the quarters into 2 neat large batons, giving 4 batons in total. Reserve the remaining pineapple for the garnish. Put the water in a jug. Put the sugar in a small heavy-bottomed saucepan over a medium heat and melt the sugar, stirring, until a deep caramel colour. Standing back, confidently pour the water onto the caramel (it will violently spit). Add the star anise and simmer until the sugar has dissolved. Put the pineapple batons into the caramel stock and simmer gently for 15 minutes, then remove from the heat and leave to cool completely. Remove the pineapple from the caramel and trim into sharp, square-edged, perfect batons, before returning to the caramel.

Shave paper-thin slices of pineapple from the reserved pineapple on a mandolin until you have 1 tablespoon per portion. Dry on kitchen (paper) towel. Place the poached pineapple and 4 handfuls of the sweet vanilla fennel on kitchen (paper) towel to dry.

Place 1 poached pineapple baton on each of 4 dessert plates. Arrange a little of the fennel salad, shaved pineapple, basil and mint on top and add a pinch of candied fennel seeds. Remove the semifreddo from the freezer, turn it out and cut into chunks. Place 3 semifreddo chunks next to the baton and arrange the fennel, pineapple, basil and mint next to it. Drizzle lightly with the vanilla syrup from the fennel and serve.

I tend not to think of making desserts as a separate way of cooking with a different set of ingredients. I view it more as cooking with ingredients that have a higher sugar content and so need higher sugar content garnishes to balance the plate. As a result, I don't view any ingredient as off limits so long as it benefits from a sweet touch. Here olive oil and rosemary slip effortlessly into a dessert context.

Serves: 4–8

CHOCOLATE OLIVE OIL POT
with rosemary soil and raspberry sorbet

FOR THE CHOCOLATE POTS
200g (7oz) dark chocolate, 53–55% cocoa solids, coarsely grated
50ml (2fl oz/scant ¼ cup) extra virgin olive oil
2g (⅓ tsp) sea salt
165ml (5½fl oz/⅔ cup) boiling water

FOR THE SORBET
450g (1lb/3⅔ cups) raspberries (fresh or frozen)
150g (5½oz/¾ cup) caster (superfine) sugar
100ml (3½fl oz/scant ½ cup) glucose syrup
200ml (7fl oz/generous ¾ cup) water
25ml (1fl oz/5 tsp) red wine vinegar
1g (⅓ tsp) xanthan gum

FOR THE ROSEMARY SOIL
50g (1¾oz/¼ cup) caster (superfine) sugar
25ml (1fl oz/5 tsp) water
50g (1¾oz) dark chocolate, 53–55% cocoa solids, coarsely grated
2g (4 tsp) rosemary leaves, finely chopped

FOR DECORATION
8–16 raspberries

First make the chocolate pots as they need 4 hours to set. Put the chocolate into the bowl of an electric mixer (or a heatproof mixing bowl) and add the olive oil and salt, then add the boiling water, which should melt the chocolate. If the chocolate doesn't melt completely, set the bowl briefly over a bain-marie (see page 188) to fully melt. Gently whisk the chocolate until it cools to 27°C/80°F or is cool to the touch. You can speed this up by placing the bowl in a larger bowl filled with cold water. When the chocolate is at the correct temperature, pour the mix into 4 to 8 pots or tea cups and put into the fridge for 4 hours to set.

Next make the raspberry sorbet. Put the raspberries, sugar, glucose syrup and measured water into a lidded saucepan. Gently bring to the boil and simmer, stirring occasionally, for about 5 minutes. Transfer the raspberry mix to a blender with the red wine vinegar and xanthan and blend until completely smooth. Sieve into a bowl and allow to cool completely. Transfer to an ice-cream maker and follow the manufacturer's instructions then store in the freezer. Otherwise see making sorbets by hand (below).

Make the rosemary soil. Put the sugar and water into a small saucepan and heat gently until it reaches 137°C/278°F. Remove from the heat, add the chocolate and rosemary and stir vigorously until the sugar crystallizes then leave to cool.

Place 1 chocolate pot on each of 4 dessert plates. Sprinkle a little of the rosemary soil onto the chocolate pot and add a pile next to the pot. Top with a scoop of sorbet, add a couple of raspberries and serve straight away.

MAKING SORBETS BY HAND

If not using an ice-cream maker, pour the sorbet mix into a 2-litre (3½-pint) container and put into the freezer. After 2 hours whisk vigorously to break up the ice crystals. Repeat every 45 minutes for up to 6 hours (depending on your freezer) until the mix is frozen through and as free from crystals as possible. Sorbets will keep in the freezer for up to 1 month.

This is a lovely dessert with some interesting flavour combinations. You may find, however, that a lot of people aren't a big fan of tarragon, especially when this concentrated. If this is the case then simply swap the tarragon for mint for an equally delicious end to a meal.

Serves: 4

POACHED PEARS
with frozen pistachio cacao cream and tarragon granita

FOR THE GRANITA
50g (1¾oz/¼ cup) caster (superfine) sugar
200ml (7fl oz/generous ¾ cup) water
20g (¾oz/½ cup) chopped tarragon

FOR THE PISTACHIO CACAO CREAM
75g (2¾oz/⅓ cup) cacao butter
165g (5¾oz/1¼ cups) Iranian pistachios
60g (2oz/⅓ cup) caster (superfine) sugar
50ml (2fl oz/scant ¼ cup) water
1 vanilla pod, halved and seeds scraped
zest of ⅛ lemon
0.5g (⅛ tsp) sea salt

FOR THE POACHED PEARS
2 ripe, firm Williams pears
250ml (8½fl oz/1 cup) white wine
125ml (4fl oz/½ cup) cold water
125g (4½oz/⅔ cups) caster (superfine) sugar
2g (1 tsp) cardamom pods
0.2g (pinch) saffron

FOR THE PEAR JELLY
250ml (8½fl oz/1 cup) poaching liquid (reserved from the pears)
vanilla pod (reserved from pistachio cacao cream), optional
2.5g (¾ tsp) iota carrageenan powder

First make the granita as it needs 4 hours to freeze. Put all the granita ingredients into a blender and blend until completely smooth. Pass through a sieve into a freezer container. Freeze for at least 4 hours until solid, then scrape with a fork to create a snow effect. Return to the freezer.

Next make the pistachio cacao cream as it needs 2 hours to freeze. Line a baking tray (sheet) with baking parchment. Melt the cacoa butter in a bain-marie (see page 188).

Set aside 15g (½oz/2 tbsp) of the pistachios. Put all the pistachio cacao butter ingredients except the reserved pistachios into a blender and blend to a very smooth cream. Spread the cream over the prepared baking tray (sheet) to a 5mm (¼-inch) thickness and sprinkle the reserved pistachios over the top. Cover with cling film (plastic wrap) and put into the freezer for 2 hours until hard. Once frozen, cut into 2–3cm (¾–1¼-inch) shards, then return to the freezer.

Prepare the poached pears. Peel the pears, cut in half lengthways, scoop out the core and cut out the woody base, leaving the stalk intact for effect. Put the rest of the poached pear ingredients into a saucepan and add the pears. Gently bring to the boil and cover with a cartouche (see page 184). Simmer until the pears are just soft (but not breaking up). Remove from the heat and leave to cool in the liquid. Strain, reserving the liquid to make the jelly, then place in the fridge.

To make the pear jelly, put the poaching liquid and vanilla pod (if using) into a small saucepan and whisk the iota in. Gently bring to the boil, whisking the whole time, then pour into a bowl. Leave to set at room temperature.

Place a pear half on each plate and then add a couple of pistachio cacao cream shards. Add 1 tablespoon of tarragon granita and a few blobs of pear jelly and serve before it melts.

I like my apple cake to be very moist and sticky, oozing caramelized sugars and apple juices everywhere. I grant you this is not very sophisticated, but it is very nice to eat. The apple and olive oil mousseline reveals one of the world's great untapped flavour combinations, apples and olive oil, while the plum purée brings vivid colour and a tangy foil to the sweet cake.

Serves: 4

MOIST APPLE CAKE
with apple mousseline and plum purée

FOR THE MOUSSELINE

6 Bramley apples, peeled, cored and cut into 1cm (½-inch) dice
25g (1oz/2 tbsp) caster (superfine) sugar
25ml (1fl oz/5 tsp) water
25ml (1fl oz/5 tsp) extra virgin olive oil

FOR THE PURÉE

250g (9oz) red-skinned plums, halved and stones removed
50g (1¾oz/¼ cup) caster (superfine) sugar
1 cinnamon stick
1 star anise
1 vanilla pod, cut in half and seeds scraped out

FOR THE SPONGE

180g (6½oz/1½ cups) plain (all-purpose) flour
4g (scant 1 tsp) bicarbonate of soda (baking soda)
5g (⅛oz/2 tsp) ground cinnamon
1g (scant ¼ tsp) sea salt
150g (5½oz/generous ¾ cup) soft brown sugar
110ml (3½fl oz/scant ½ cup) extra virgin olive oil
55ml (2fl oz/¼ cup) water
15ml (1 tbsp) cider vinegar
4 large Bramley apples, peeled, cored and cut into 1cm (½-inch) dice
50g (1¾oz/¼ cup) demerara sugar

First make the mousseline as it takes 4 hours to set. Place the diced apple in a saucepan with the sugar and water. Cook gently until the apples break down. Transfer to a blender and process to a smooth purée. Clean out the saucepan and return the apple mix. Cook until the apple becomes thick and gloopy, then remove from the heat. Using a wire whisk, whisk in the olive oil to give a glossy texture. Transfer to a small container and cover with cling film (plastic wrap), in contact with the surface, and leave to cool. Place in the fridge for 4 hours to become very firm.

To make the plum purée, in a bowl mix together the plum halves, sugar, cinnamon, star anise, vanilla pod and seeds. Place a 45cm (18-inch) strip of foil over a deep baking tray (sheet) and cover with a 45cm (18-inch) strip of baking parchment, forming a well in the middle. Put the plum mix into the well. Fold the tin foil/paper in half and roll up the edges to form a sealed parcel. Bake for 20 minutes then remove from the oven and allow to cool completely before opening. Remove the cinnamon, vanilla pod and star anise, then transfer the plums and liquid to a blender. Blend on full speed until the mix is completely smooth. Strain through a sieve and place in the fridge.

Next make the cake. Preheat the oven to (fan) 140°C/160°C/310°F/gas mark 2½. Grease and line a 20cm (8-inch) square, loose-bottomed baking tin (pan). Mix the flour, bicarbonate of soda (baking soda), cinnamon, salt and brown sugar together in a large bowl. In a jug, mix the olive oil, water and cider vinegar together, then pour it into the flour mix. Using a spoon, mix gently until just combined – don't beat. Fold the diced apple in until well combined. Pour the mix into the prepared baking tin (pan) and level out. Sprinkle with the demerara sugar and bake for 30–40 minutes until the top is golden and it is cooked through (check by inserting a cocktail stick into the centre – it should come out clean). Leave to cool for 10 minutes, then remove from the tin (pan) and leave on a cooling rack until cold.

When ready to serve, slice the apple sponge. Place a slice of cake on each of 4 dessert plates. Drizzle 2 tablespoons of plum purée around each plate, then add a scoop of apple mousseline and serve.

BREADS

A good rye bread is an essential recipe to have in your repertoire. The base of this recipe is a sour dough, which may make you worry it's going to be complicated, but the truth is it's the opposite. You have to give a little more forethought, thinking in days not hours, but sourdoughs are gentle creatures and can be easily sped up or slowed down with temperature changes.

Making the initial sour dough mix does take a while (five days to be exact), but it also takes just a minute or two a day; and once you have your "mother" you can just keep it rolling over, time after time.

Makes: 1 loaf

RYE BREAD

FOR THE RYE BREAD STARTER
| Day 1 |

50g (1¾oz/scant ½ cup)
   wholemeal (wholewheat)
   rye flour
100ml (3½fl oz/scant ½ cup)
   warm water (40°C/104°F)

| Days 2, 3 and 4 |

25g (1oz/scant ¼ cup) wholemeal
   (wholewheat) rye flour
50ml (2fl oz/scant ¼ cup) warm
   water (40°C/104°F)

| For the "mother" |

50g (1¾oz) rye bread starter (or
   reserved "mother")
175g (6¼oz/1½ cups) wholemeal
   (wholewheat) rye flour
350ml (12fl oz/1½ cups) warm
   water (40°C/104°F)

FOR THE RYE BREAD
450g (1lb) of "the mother" (see
   above)
345g (12oz/scant 3 cups)
   wholemeal (wholewheat) rye
   flour
3g (1½ tsp) caraway seeds
   (optional)
8g (¼oz/1½ tsp) sea salt
200ml (7fl oz/generous ¾ cup)
   water

On Day 1, mix the rye flour and water together in a small very clean container or jar and loosely place a lid on it (so air can get in). Leave in a warm place (around 22°C/71°F).

On Days 2, 3 and 4, add the rye flour and water to the mix each day, return the lid and place back in the warm place.

On Day 5 your mix should be bubbly and smell sweetly sour. It may have fermented, in which case it will appear separated with a liquid layer, but as long as it smells sweet and/or sour it will be ok. If it is mouldy or smells unpleasant then you'll have to throw it away and start again. If it isn't bubbling or smells like flour then it wasn't kept in a warm enough place – discard three-quarters of the mix and carry on adding flour and water for a few more days making sure it is kept in a warm enough place.

When the mix is ready you can create your yeast culture, the "mother". Mix all the "mother" ingredients together in a bowl. Cover with a tea towel and put somewhere warm for about 12 hours.

Now you can make the rye bread. Line a 900g (2lb) loaf tin (pan) with baking parchment. Weigh 450g (1lb) of the "mother" into a large bowl and keep the rest to refresh the "mother" (see box, below). Add the rest of the ingredients and stir to form a clay-like mix. Spoon into the prepared loaf tin (pan) – it should fill two-thirds of it – and smooth the top. Cover with cling film (plastic wrap) and put somewhere warm for 4–5 hours until risen to the top of the loaf tin (pan).

Preheat the oven to (fan) 170°C/190°C/375°F/gas mark 5. Remove the cling film (plastic wrap) and bake the bread for 45 minutes to 1 hour. When you think it's ready, remove from the tin (pan) and tap the bottom of the loaf, it should give a dull hollow thud. If it doesn't, bake for 20 more minutes. Allow to cool for 4 hours before cutting.

THE "MOTHER"

The remaining "mother" can either have flour and water added to make bread again the next day, or you can put it in an airtight container in the fridge where it will keep for up to 1 month until you next want to make bread.

Sometimes it is good to have a cracker that has a bit of character of its own. So often a cracker is just a vehicle to get whatever you've spread on it into your mouth, but not in this case. These traditional Scandinavian crackers are best paired with quite neutral pâtés and dips, anything too strong and the flavours may compete. If you want something with a little less character then simply omit the caraway seeds.

Makes 20 crisp breads

RYE CRISP BREADS

65g (2oz/½ cup) dark rye flour, plus extra to dust
65g (2oz/½ cup) wholemeal (wholewheat) spelt flour (or plain wholemeal/wholewheat flour)
10g (¼oz/1 tbsp) flax seeds
10g (¼oz/1¼ tbsp) sesame seeds
2g (1 tsp) caraway seeds
3g (½ tsp) sea salt
3g (¾ tsp) dried yeast
90ml (3¼fl oz/generous ⅓ cup) warm water (40°C/104°F)

Put all the ingredients in a bowl and bring together into a rough dough. Transfer to a clean work surface and knead for 5 minutes until the dough is smooth. Put back into the bowl and cover with cling film (plastic wrap). Place in a cool place (20°C/68°F) for at least 2 hours, but ideally 12–24 hours (the longer you leave it, the better it will taste).

Preheat the oven to (fan) 160°C/180°C/350°F/gas mark 4.

Dust your work surface with rye flour and divide the dough into 4. Roll each batch out as thin as you can – the thinner you roll it, the crisper the bread will be.

Cut the mix into your desired shape. I either make random shards approximately 5cm (2 inches) long or use a cookie cutter to get a neat round circular shape.

Line a baking tray (sheet) with non-stick baking parchment and arrange the crisp breads neatly on it, shaking as much flour from them as you can. Bake until golden and crisp – this will take up to 10 minutes, depending on how thin you rolled them.

Remove from the oven and allow to cool. These will keep for up to 4 weeks in an airtight container.

When I discovered the book *Tartine Bread*, by Chad Robertson, where he recommends using a Dutch oven (a sort of lidded cast-iron saucepan) for baking bread, my life was changed for ever. This allows the heat and moisture of the loaf to be kept close while baking to create a wonderful deep crust. This loaf is designed to be quick and reliable, but if you want to learn the true detail of using a Dutch oven then I cannot recommend Chad's book enough.

This recipe will also work well without the yeast, but you will have to extend the initial proving time from one hour to over four hours, and the second prove from 45 minutes to over two hours. If you are not using a Dutch oven, then just use a baking tray (sheet), preheated in the same way.

Makes: 1 loaf

EVERYDAY BREAD

FOR THE RYE SOUR DOUGH
100g (3½oz) retained rye bread
    sour dough "mother" (see
    page 209)
100g (3½oz/¾ cup) dark rye flour
200ml (7fl oz/generous ¾ cup)
    water

FOR THE EVERYDAY BREAD
275g (9¾oz) rye bread sour dough
    from above (use the remaining
    mix for your next "mother")
640g (1lb 7oz/4½ cups) organic
    strong white bread flour, plus
    extra to dust
250ml (8½fl oz/1 cup) warm water
    (40°C/104°F)
10g (¼oz/1¾ tsp) sea salt
6g (⅛oz/1½ tsp) dried yeast
    (optional)

Mix all the ingredients for the rye sour dough together in a bowl, cover with a clean tea towel and leave in a warm place (about 22°C/71°F) overnight.

Preheat the oven to (fan) 200°C/220°C/425°F/gas mark 7.

Put all the ingredients for the everyday bread into a large bowl and bring together to make a dough using a dough scraper. Turn the mix out onto a clean work surface and knead for 10 minutes until the dough is glossy and smooth. Return the mix to the bowl, cover with a clean tea towel and leave for 1 hour until doubled in size.

Turn the dough out onto a work surface dusted with a little flour and flatten to a large square shape. Bring one corner over to the middle and push it down to stick it in place, turn the dough and bring the next corner into the middle. Keep repeating this process going round and round the dough, at least 6 times, until a ball has formed with a tight gluten skin stretched over it.

Dust a large proving basket (or mixing bowl lined with a tea towel) with semolina and put the dough into the basket. Leave to prove for 45 minutes or until nearly doubled in size. If you are using a Dutch oven, put it into the oven, frying pan (skillet) side down, at the point when you set the dough aside to rise. Otherwise heat a baking tray (sheet).

Once the dough is ready, remove the Dutch oven from the oven and remove the heavy lid. Turn the proving basket over onto the base of the Dutch oven, trying not to knock too much air out. Using a sharp bread knife (or razor blade for an authentic experience), cut 4 x 1cm (½ inch) deep slashes in the top.

Put the top back on the Dutch oven and put it into the oven for 20 minutes. After 20 minutes carefully remove the top of the Dutch oven and turn the oven down to (fan) 160°C/180°C/350°F/gas mark 4. Bake for a further 30 minutes until golden brown with a good crust. If not using a Dutch oven, cook for the same times as above, turning the oven down after 20 minutes.

Remove from the oven and leave to cool on a cooling rack, then enjoy.

This Sardinian bread is supposed to be so thin before it's baked that you can read your music through it. I find it a great, crispy cracker to spread creamy pâtés on. Once made, the carta di musica will last a long time, provided they are kept dry, and are a handy bread to have to hand should you need an emergency cracker. I like to roll the dough through a pasta machine to ensure an even, ultra-thin end result, but you can roll it out by hand using a more traditional rolling pin and floured surface should you wish.

Serves: 8–12

CARTA DI MUSICA

100g (3½oz/scant ¾ cup) type 00 flour
90g (3oz/½ cup) fine semolina, plus extra to dust
2g (½ tsp) dried yeast
2g (⅓ tsp) sea salt
100ml (3½fl oz/scant ½ cup) water
extra virgin olive oil
coarse grain salt

Place the flour, semolina, dried yeast and sea salt in a bowl and add the water. Knead for about 2 minutes to make a smooth dough, then leave to rest in a warm place (about 22°C/71°F) for 1 hour to rise. Knock it back by kneading and punching the air out, then turn it out onto a work surface. Knead for 5 more minutes to achieve a supple elastic dough. Leave somewhere warm for 45 minutes to rise.

Preheat the oven to (fan) 160°C/180°C/350°F/gas mark 4.

If using a pasta machine, knock the dough back and cut it in half. Using the pasta machine, process half the dough at a time, as for pasta (see page 126), working down through the settings until it has gone through the second to last setting.

If using a rolling pin, knock it back and cut it into 6 balls. Roll out 1 ball as thinly as you can without the dough breaking.

Spread your rolled dough out on a clean work surface lightly dusted with semolina. Using a sharp knife cut the mix into 3cm (1¼-inch) strips along its width. Lay these strips out on a large baking tray (sheet) and bake in the oven for 5 minutes. You want them to puff up and cook but not go crispy. Remove from the oven and lay them out on your work surface.

Using a large flat surface, like a chopping board, squash the breads flat, applying a fair bit of pressure. Brush each bread lightly with olive oil using a pastry brush, and sprinkle a little coarse salt on top. Put the breads back onto the baking tray (sheet) and return to the oven for 5 more minutes until golden brown and crisp. Repeat with the rest of the mix.

When cool, these can be kept in an airtight container for up to 4 weeks.

This is a very quick bread to make and a great accompaniment to a wide variety of dishes. If you want to add another level of interest, sprinkle the breads with pistachio dukkah (see page 114), chilli flakes (crushed chillies) or herbs just after you drizzle them with olive oil.

Makes: 6

FLAT BREADS

335g (11½oz/2⅓ cups) type 00 flour (or strong white bread flour), plus extra to dust
7g (¼oz/1¼ tsp) sea salt
7g (¼oz/1¾ tsp) dried yeast
30ml (1fl oz/2 tbsp) extra virgin olive oil, plus extra to drizzle
215ml (7½fl oz/scant 1 cup) water

Place the flour, salt and yeast in a large bowl. Place the olive oil and water in a jug and mix with a fork, then pour into the dry ingredients. Mix with a dough scraper or spoon to form a rough dough, then turn out onto a clean work surface.

Knead the dough for about 8 minutes until soft and supple, then return to the bowl and cover with cling film (plastic wrap). Leave to prove somewhere warm for about 1 hour until it has doubled in size. Turn the dough out onto the work surface and knead for 2 minutes. Form into a ball and cut in half, then cut each half into thirds and dust lightly with flour.

Push each piece flat onto the work surface to form a disc and then fold one edge into the middle. Press it down with your thumb to stick, and turn the disc round a few centimetres (an inch). Bring the edge into the middle again and stick again. You will see a gluten layer stretching across the dough. Keep lifting, sticking and turning, going round 2 or 3 times, until the dough resembles a firm ball. Repeat for all the pieces and leave to rest, crease side down, for 15 minutes covered with a clean tea towel.

Lightly dust the work surface with flour and place one ball on it with the creased side down. Flatten with the palm of your hand, then, with a rolling pin, roll the dough to a circle 20–25cm (8–10 inches) wide. Using your fingers, stretch out the edges of the bread to thicken them slightly (like you would for pizza dough). Dust the dough with flour and set aside. Repeat for each ball of dough and leave for 20 minutes to rest.

Heat a large, heavy-based griddle pan until very hot (but not burning hot). Turn the temperature down to medium. Add one of the flat breads and cook until the underside is golden and the top has bubbled and puffed up. Flip the bread over and cook the other side for 2 minutes. Remove to a plate, bubbly side up, and drizzle lightly with olive oil and any other herbs you wish (see introduction, above). Repeat for each flat bread. Serve warm.

This bread is moist, moreish and decadent, but often it gets made mainly because it is so quick to prepare. Don't let this put you off, though, it is really delicious in its own right, but it is quick to make, and that is important to remember.

Makes: 1 focaccia

FOCCACIA

500g (1lb 2oz/3½ cups) type 00 flour (or strong white bread flour), plus extra to dust
25g (1oz/2½ tbsp) fine semolina
10g (¼oz/2½ tsp) dried yeast
13g (⅓oz/2½ tsp) sea salt
320ml (10½fl oz/1⅓ cups) warm water (40°C/104°F)
35ml (1fl oz/7 tsp) extra virgin olive oil, plus extra to grease
40ml (1½fl oz/8 tsp) top-quality extra virgin olive oil
20g (¾oz/3½ tsp) sea salt flakes

Mix the flour, semolina, dried yeast and 8g (¼oz/1½ tsp) of salt together in a bowl. Add the water and regular olive oil and mix together to form a rough dough. Turn the dough out onto a clean work surface lightly dusted with flour and knead for 10 minutes until the dough is smooth, soft and supple.

Grease a 17 x 25 x 2cm (7 x 10 x ¾ inch) ceramic roasting dish with olive oil. Fold your dough over twice to get a smooth top and then roll or press into a rough rectangle the size of your roasting dish. Put the dough into the dish and stretch to fill it to the edges. Cover with a clean tea towel and place somewhere a little warmer than room temperature for about an hour – it needs to have risen to the top of the tray.

Preheat the oven to (fan) 160°C/180°C/350°F/gas mark 4.

Poke your fingers into the dough in 2 x 4 rows to create the characteristic dimples, making sure you touch the bottom of the dish when you poke each hole. Sprinkle the dough with the remaining 5g (⅛oz/1 tsp) of salt.

Bake in the oven for 30–40 minutes until golden and risen. Remove from the oven and immediately drizzle the top-quality olive oil evenly over the top and sprinkle with the sea salt flakes. Leave to cool for 5 minutes and then transfer to a cooling rack and allow to cool completely.

| OILS, BUTTERS AND MILKS |

FENUGREEK OIL

Using this oil is a great way to add a subtle depth and interest to a dish without dominating it. This goes especially well with garlic and onion flavours and is a surprising partner for truffle.

Makes: 150ml (5fl oz/⅔ cup)

10g (¼oz/scant 1 tbsp) fenugreek seeds
150ml (5fl oz/⅔ cup) rapeseed oil

Put the fenugreek seeds and oil in a small saucepan and heat gently to 80°C/176°F. Remove from the heat, allow to cool, then transfer to a sealed bottle. Store for at least 2 weeks before using.

This will keep in the fridge for 3 months.

THYME OIL

This is a great way to add a little herbaceous interest to a dish without overwhelming it with greenery. It is also good to dip bread into, should the fancy take you.

Makes: 125ml (4fl oz/½ cup)

10g (¼oz) sprigs of thyme
1 small shallot, sliced
1 clove of garlic, peeled
1 dried red chilli
1 bay leaf, torn
5 peppercorns
125ml (4fl oz/½ cup) extra virgin olive oil

Put all the ingredients into a small saucepan. Very gently heat until the shallots begin to bubble. Remove from the heat and leave to cool.

Transfer to a jar and push down the solid ingredients so they are covered by oil. Leave for at least 8 hours, and ideally up to 2 weeks, to infuse. After 14 days strain the oil and discard the solids.

This will keep in the fridge for 3 months.

GARLIC PARSLEY OIL

This is an immensely useful thing to have in the fridge. Whenever you want to add a bit of depth to a dish just sprinkle this in, cook for a few minutes, and it will make it instantly delicious.

Makes: 200ml (7fl oz/generous ¾ cup)

10 cloves of garlic, peeled
15g (½oz/4 tbsp) parsley leaves, roughly chopped
175ml (6fl oz/¾ cup) extra virgin olive oil

Put all the ingredients into a blender and process until smooth.

This will keep in an airtight container in the fridge for up to 1 month.

LAVENDER OIL

You have to be a little careful with lavender. Just the right amount brings a subtle sophistication to a dish, but even a touch too much and it will make it taste like medicine. You want this oil to be obviously lavender flavoured but not bitter or overwhelming.

Makes: 125ml (4fl oz/½ cup)

10g (¼oz) sprigs of thyme
3g (4 tsp) dried lavender
125ml (4fl oz/½ cup) rapeseed oil

Put all the ingredients into a small saucepan and heat gently until the thyme just begins to bubble. Remove from the heat and leave to infuse for 4 hours. Taste, and if the lavender is pronounced but not overwhelming, strain. If not ready, leave a little longer and re-test, then strain.

This will keep in the fridge for 3 months.

PINE NUT BUTTER

This recipe is essential to producing elegant, artisan, plant-based food in the Italian tradition. The creamy moreishness of pine nuts combined with the buttery overtones of olive oil give this fridge staple essential status. If you are making it just for one recipe then simply make one batch, but I always multiply this recipe by at least four to have some to hand.

Makes: 175g (6¼oz)

100g (3½oz/¾ cup) pine nuts
25ml (1fl oz/5 tsp) Italian extra virgin olive oil
  (preferably Sicilian)
75ml (2¾fl oz/⅓ cup) water

Preheat the oven to (fan) 160°C/180°C/350°F/gas mark 4.

Put the pine nuts on a small baking tray (sheet) and roast in the oven for no more than 3 minutes – you are warming them, not colouring them.

Put the pine nuts, olive oil and water into a blender and blend until silky smooth. Pass through a sieve and store in a container.

This will keep in the fridge for up to 7 days.

HAZELNUT BUTTER

I use this in the baked potato croquetas (see page 160) to bring both nuttiness and a luxurious richness.

Makes: 220g (8oz)

110g (3¾oz/¾ cup) blanched hazelnuts
30ml (1fl oz/2 tbsp) hazelnut oil
85ml (2¾fl oz/⅓ cup) water
2.5g (scant ½ tsp) sea salt
2.5g (generous ½ tsp) caster (superfine) sugar

Preheat the oven to (fan) 160°C/180°C/350°F/gas mark 4.

Put the hazelnuts onto a small baking tray (sheet) and roast in the oven for 7 minutes until golden.

Put the roasted hazelnuts and the rest of the ingredients into a blender and blend until very smooth. This will keep in the fridge for up to 3 days.

ALMOND MILK

This recipe contains nothing but almonds, so all the body and flavour comes from the almond mass alone. Although this makes a thick milk, you can add up to double the water for a lighter version.

Makes: 250ml (8½fl oz/1 cup)

100g (3½oz/scant ¾ cup) whole almonds
300ml (10fl oz/1¼ cups) cold water

Put the almonds into a small bowl, cover with cold water by at least 2.5cm (1 inch), and put into the fridge overnight. When ready to make the milk, drain the almonds and rinse well. Transfer the almonds to a blender and add the measured water. Process for 1–2 minutes until smooth and creamy.

Line a sieve with a 45cm (18-inch) square piece of sterile muslin (cheesecloth) and set over a jug. Pour the mix into the muslin (cheesecloth) and collect up the corners to make a bag. Squeeze the bag to extract the milk into the jug until you are struggling to get much liquid.

The almond milk will keep in the fridge for up to 3 days.

SMOKED HAZELNUT MILK

This simple variation on nut milk adds a savoury depth wherever it is used, either as the base for a sauce or the sauce itself.

Makes: 200ml (7fl oz/generous ¾ cup)

80g (2¾oz/scant ⅔ cup) hazelnuts
200ml (7fl oz/generous ¾ cup) water
10ml (2 tsp) hazelnut oil
sea salt

Put 1 tbsp of hickory chips into a stove-top smoker. Line the top grate with foil to prevent the nuts from escaping, and follow the manufacturer's instructions. Smoke the nuts until they have a light smoky flavour.

Transfer the nuts to a blender with the water and oil and blend to a paste. Follow the method for almond milk (see above) to strain the milk through a muslin (cheesecloth), then season to taste. It should be rich, nutty and smoky. This will keep in the fridge for up to 3 days.

INDEX

ACKNOWLEDGEMENTS

Helen – I am only one half of everything we achieve, you have always been there, you cared for our family, tidied in my wake, ran the errands, picked up the pieces and kept me going whenever I wanted to stop. Nothing could have happened without you.

My parents – For always supporting me, for always being there and for always believing, even when you probably thought you shouldn't.

Rachel and Keith – For always being there when we needed you, for going above and beyond every day to help, just so I can make some vegetables hot.

Jo Edwards Castle Farm Organics – We have worked together for ten years now and without your perfectly wonky vegetables I could never have produced the food I have. Thank you for inviting us onto your farm for the photo shoot, rushing around finding "two leaves of this" and "another one of that but muddier", for helping to clean, providing tea and keeping me going. This book is as much about your farm as my food.

Over the years I have worked with too many amazing people to mention, needless to say I learnt something from every one of them and there is a piece of them all on every page of this book.

To the current chefs in the restaurant: Steve, Jamie, Jake, Jerome and Alfie – Thank you for not shouting when I stole your prep, pinched your deliveries and dumped my washing-up after a long day. Your skill and dedication never fails to inspire me.

Kev – Thank you for quietly keeping it all going and making it better.

Suresh – For having the patience to convince me this was a good idea and gently steering the ship.

Fritha – For seeing something and for gently and politely keeping everything on the straight and narrow.

A book is only partly about the recipes and the writing. Kim, your photographs make this book what it is. Tania, you have worked with endless changes in brief, edits and reshuffles and didn't swear at me once. Claire, for helping to turn what I think is right into what is better. Caroline, for endlessly wandering the south-west to find just the perfect plate. Silvana, for lending us your beautiful things at a moment's notice and never once complaining.

With thanks for the loan of ceramics to Elvis Robertson Ceramics, elvisrobertson.com, pages 23, 24, 51, 71, 80, 83, 145, 148, 152, 173, 203, 205; residentstove.co.uk, page 86.

AUTHOR BIOGRAPHY

Richard is chef–proprietor of the award-winning Acorn Vegetarian Kitchen in Bath, UK. Placing vegetables at the centre of the plate, the restaurant is frequently mentioned as among the UK and the world's top vegetarian eateries.

Richard was raised a vegetarian and, after graduating with a 1:1 degree in English Literature, he set about studying vegetable cookery while working in a series of top vegetarian restaurants. This culminated in his five-year role as head chef for Demuth's Restaurant where he developed and refined his plant-centric, cooking style.

He has a passion for sharing the knowledge and techniques that he has learnt and developed in order to increase the standard of plant-based food across the country.

OVS

15.